The Twin Thing

'We have that twin thing going on. Wherever we are in the world, we kind of know what the other one's doing.' –
Sia Barbi.

'That's right. It's instinctive. It's a twin thing.' –
Shane Barbi.

(quoted in *Sunday Telegraph Magazine*, 9 June 2002)

Also by Guy Lyon Playfair:

The Flying Cow
The Indefinite Boundary
The Cycles of Heaven (with Scott Hill)
This House is Haunted
If This Be Magic
The Haunted Pub Guide
The Geller Effect (with Uri Geller)
A Question of Memory (with David Berglas)
The Evil Eye
Mindforce

Twin Telepathy
The Psychic Connection

Guy Lyon Playfair

Vega 2002
Text © Guy Lyon Playfair 2002

ISBN 1-84333-686-3

A catalogue record for this book is available
from the British Library

First published in 2002 by
Vega
64 Brewery Road
London, N7 9NT

A member of **Chrysalis** Books plc

Visit our website at www.chrysalisbooks.co.uk

Printed in Great Britain
by CPD, Wales

CONTENTS

CONTENTS

ACKNOWLEDGEMENTS

I am most grateful to the librarians and staff of the British Library, the College of Psychic Studies, Imperial College and Science Museum Library, Kensington and Chelsea Public Library, the London Library, the Parapsychology Foundation, the Royal Society, the Royal Society of Medicine, St Thomas's Hospital Medical School and the Society for Psychical Research.

Thanks also to all those without whose help, encouragement, criticism of early drafts, and above all supply of original case material, this book could not have been written: Shari Andrews, Dr Alison Armour, Aileen Biggs, Iosif Boczor, Dawn Booth-Clibbon, Bernard Carr, Dr Shari Cohn, Dr Ian Fletcher, Uri Geller, Joanna Gray, Barbara Herbert, Michèle Koralek, Tina Laurent, David Lorimer, Alasdair McWhirter, Sophia and Meena Mohammad, Simon Pettet, John and Line Playfair, Susan Podesta-Oliver, Anna Powles, Hana-Maria Pravda, Mahbuba Rahmany, John L. Randall, Steve Roberts, Audrey Sandbank, Alexander Timoschenko, Lawrence Wright and Tony Zacharias.

Special thanks to Dr Rupert Sheldrake and Colin Wilson for their valuable contributions and to Stuart Booth, without whose initial encouragement this book might never have been written, let alone published.

Special thanks also to copy editors Sarah Barlow and Rob Dimery for tying up so many of my loose ends.

G.L.P.

FOREWORD BY DR RUPERT SHELDRAKE

Like many other people, I have long been fascinated by stories of telepathy between identical twins. For many years I have been looking in vain for authoritative research on this intriguing subject. At last I have found it in this book.

Guy Lyon Playfair is admirably qualified for this study. He is one of the world's leading psychical researchers, has an extraordinarily wide knowledge of the field, and is very well informed about the history of the subject. This book summarizes research on twins over more than one hundred years, and shows how strong the evidence is for telepathy between identical twins, and indeed for telepathy in general.

Of course, not all twins are telepathic, and even those that are do not show telepathy all the time. Playfair shows that about 30 to 35 per cent of identical twins have experienced telepathy and he examines the conditions under which this telepathy appears. His conclusions illuminate the nature of telepathy in general, which depends on close bonds between the 'sender' and 'receiver'.

Close bonds conducive to telepathy also occur between people and animals. I myself have done extensive research on telepathy between people and pets such as dogs and cats (summarized in my book *Dogs That Know When Their Owners Are Coming Home*). The telepathic abilities of a range of animal species provide strong evidence that telepathy is a biological phenomenon, rather than a specifically human one. I have also recently been carrying out research on telepathy between mothers and babies, where the bonds are normally strong and telepathy is relatively common. But whereas people's relationships with their pets are fairly short-lived because dogs and cats generally have much shorter lives than people, and whereas relations with mothers and babies are short-lived because babies grow up, relationships between twins can be life-long. Twins therefore provide some of the best opportunities for studying person-to-person telepathy.

In the final chapter Playfair discusses the principle of non-locality in quantum physics, according to which two systems that have been linked together in the past retain a non-local connection. He shows how this could be very relevant to the understanding of telepathy between monozygotic twins, who were once part of the same fertilized egg cell. His discussion also reminds us that non-local connections are already part of mainstream physics, and no longer seem as outrageous or impossible as they did in the heyday of materialism, when many of the still-prevalent prejudices against telepathy developed.

It is remarkable that such an interesting subject should have been so little investigated. The fact that Playfair's comprehensive review is so brief is a testimony to this state of affairs. But in some ways the underdeveloped state of research in this field is an advantage. In most areas of science, it is difficult to see the wood for the trees. There are simply too many details. This is not the case for research on telepathy in general and the connections between twins in particular. This is a field of research still in its infancy. As a result, at the beginning of the 21st century much unexplored territory still lies open before us, providing remarkable opportunities to learn about the nature of the mind and about human nature itself. Playfair suggests a number of ways in which new enquiries could be undertaken, and I hope that this timely book will act as a stimulus for long-overdue research.

INTRODUCTION BY COLIN WILSON

It may seem an odd thing to say, but I owe an immense debt of gratitude to Guy Lyon Playfair for teaching me just how little I knew about the paranormal. This is how it came about.

Whilst it is true that I had been fascinated by spiritualism as a child, this interest had simply evaporated before I reached my teens, when I began to study science. By the time I was 14, I was just about as sceptical as it is possible to be.

Later, in 1953, when I was 22, I was swept away by the then new philosophy called existentialism that had been imported into the UK from Paris at the end of the Second World War. It was my starting point in my first book, *The Outsider*, which was published in 1956. This only strengthened my basic scepticism in what Albert Camus called 'beyonds'.

Then, in 1969, an American publisher asked me if I could write a book called *The Occult*. Because my attitudes were more or less still as described above, it was not a subject on which I was well informed. Furthermore, I am ashamed to say that I hardly noticed the 1960s, living in the depths of Cornwall and too busy trying to earn a living as a full-time writer as breadwinner and husband. The fact that the world had become interested in the likes of yoga, magic and the paranormal had simply passed me by.

It was when collecting material for *The Occult* that things began to change. My wife showed me a passage from a book she was reading, *Left Hand, Right Hand*, the autobiography of Sir Osbert Sitwell. It described how he and a young bunch of fellow officers had consulted a well-known palmist. Hoping to learn about their love lives and financial prospects, they had been disconcerted by the bewildered reaction of the hand reader. To every one of them she had cried out, 'I can't understand it. The life line stops after a few months and I cannot read anything.' The officers assumed this was a mere excuse. Yet, a few months later, the First World War broke out, and all the officers were killed at the front.

I was impressed. I knew Sitwell was a hard-headed sceptic, who, like his father, had a habit of exposing fake mediums. Further, as I continued researching my book, I found more and more similar stories that had the ring of truth. Soon, I came to accept that there were such things as 'paranormal powers'.

Yet, although these powers included telepathy, clairvoyance and precognition, or an ability to foresee the future, I continued to be dubious about such aspects as ghosts, in particular, and spirits of the dead in general. And when it came to poltergeists, I had no doubt that the Freudian investigator Nandor Fodor had stumbled upon the truth about these 'banging ghosts' when he concluded that they were due to the unconscious repressions of psychologically disturbed teenagers.

Indeed, I still wince when I recall assuring a girl that I met in a BBC canteen in Bristol that the poltergeist who kept setting alight her clothes in the wardrobe was caused by her own unconscious mind. And this when I was actually making a programme for BBC Television about a poltergeist case!

Nevertheless, I was sufficiently intrigued by another poltergeist case in Pontefract, Yorkshire, to think there may be material for a book about it all. So, in late August 1968, I decided to see for myself and en route was invited to lecture on the paranormal at the Hayes Conference Centre at Swanwick in Derbyshire. It was a significant point in my life, for I noted that one of my fellow speakers was to be Guy Lyon Playfair.

It was our first meeting and I explained that after the talk I was going on to a poltergeist investigation in Yorkshire and asked him, casually, what he thought poltergeists might be.

He told me that nobody really knew, but a theory he had heard from a gypsy was as good as any. This involved, among other things, 'footballs' of energy which condense into pools of water on the floor.

INTRODUCTION

It was fascinating stuff, but it was only when actually at the Pontefract case the next day that I was fully hooked. I had asked one of the people there how it had first started. 'Well, there were these odd pools of water on the kitchen floor...' I remembered in an instant what Guy had said and realized he knew more about such matters than I ever would.

On returning home to Cornwall, I settled down to read all of Guy's books in chronological order. There were half a dozen or so – and all are classics in the field of paranormal research. I was even more impressed and arranged to meet him again, this time in London, and recorded at length all of what he knew about the paranormal and how he became involved in its research. When he went on to tell of amazing paranormal experiences and adventures during his years in Brazil, I could appreciate the basis of what was the true nature of the paranormal.

However, I could also see the problem in getting the ideas across to a wider, and doubting audience. While we are perfectly willing to accept the existence of such things as quarks, black holes and a hundred things of which we have no direct experience, we draw the line at anything that sounds like old-fashioned superstition. The figure of the dotty medium – like Noel Coward's Madame Arcati in *Blithe Spirit* – still detracts from the idea of paranormal research and prevents many of us from understanding half of what is going on in our universe.

So, whilst such notions still often sound incredible to the so-called sophisticated Western reader, Guy accepts these concepts openly. He has seen them in practice, especially when he was in Brazil, as part of everyday experience.

He knows what he is talking about and that is why I found reading his books to be such a mental revolution and his work so refreshing. He is a university-trained investigator, a rather modest, quiet person and probably the last person in the world one would expect to believe in 'spirits'. (He looks pained, though, if I use the word 'spirits' when talking to him, for he prefers to call them 'entities', insisting that 'spirits' makes it sound as if we are confining the term to spirits of the dead.) He expresses the case for the paranormal – psychic powers and presences, telepathy and so forth – with a clarity and common sense that I find exhilarating.

I read *Twin Telepathy* with complete fascination. Like all Guy's books, it is marvellously researched and written in an easygoing, very readable – and often amusing – style. It will obviously become a classic of psychical research. Naturally, given its overriding subject matter, it is much preoccupied with telepathy; but it also moves into far stranger fields. For example:

A young man skiing in the Alps falls and breaks a leg. At exactly the same time, his twin brother on another piste falls and breaks his leg – the same leg, in the same place, and again at exactly the same time. This seems absurd, yet it suggests that there are underlying connections in the universe that cannot be explained in terms of the laws of physics, and to which Jung applied the term 'synchronicity'.

Charles Darwin's contemporary and co-discoverer of evolution, Alfred Russel Wallace said, 'If you leave out all the spiritual nature of man, you are not studying man at all.' Similarly, the late Glen Schaefer, Professor of Ecological Physics at Cranfield University in the UK, is quoted as saying, 'Intelligence dominates the entire universe and the whole of evolution.' Such views would, of course, horrify most professors of biology, who would dismiss them as 'teleology' – the fancy of thinking that natural processes have a 'purpose'. Yet, it is to that proposition that Guy Lyon Playfair has dedicated most of his life's work. In my view, that makes him one of the great paranormal investigators of all time.

CHAPTER 1

THIS DAFT QUESTION

Early in the evening of 27 November 1975, the writer and television personality Ross McWhirter was shot in the head and chest by two gunmen on the doorstep of his north London home. He was rushed to hospital, but was declared dead on or shortly after arrival, before his identical twin brother Norris could reach his bedside. The murder made the front pages of the following day's newspapers, for the McWhirters, editors of the *Guinness Book of Records*, were probably Britain's best-known pair of twins after the notorious criminal Kray brothers (of whom more anon).[1]

When I heard the news on the radio that night I found myself wondering if there was any truth in the claim that twins could pick up each other's thoughts and feelings at a distance. I had read somewhere that telepathy – the receiving of information by other than our normal five senses – was common between twins, especially at times of crisis, and since murder is the most extreme crisis imaginable, I thought here was a good opportunity to put that theory to the test.

The problem was that I did not know Norris McWhirter, and did not feel like writing to ask what, if anything, he felt when Ross was killed. I did, however, eagerly read his biographical tribute to Ross, which was published the following year,[2] but finding that there was no mention of telepathy in it, I decided that while some twins might be telepathic, these two had not been. Even so, the incident stuck in my mind, and I began asking around in the hope of finding somebody who knew Norris well enough to ask him, after a decent interval, if he had experienced anything at the time of Ross's death. I thought that he might have, but had preferred not to mention it in his book. However, I could not find anybody who knew him at all, so it seemed there was nothing more I could do.

Fortunately, I was wrong. More than 20 years later I had one of those lucky breaks that make you think you do have a guardian angel after all. As I will describe in more detail in due course, I was able to get an eye-witness account from somebody who had been with Norris McWhirter at the time of the shooting and yes, he had unmistakably reacted. Moreover, he had reacted in a dramatic way, almost as if he too had been shot – by an invisible bullet. So it seemed there could be a special twin connection after all.

I decided it was time for some proper research into it.

I published four appeals for evidence, and asked everybody I met if they knew any twins. Early results were disappointing – the only twins I knew or was able to meet had never had any experience of the sort I was looking for, and I received fewer replies than I had hoped. Even so, the evidence began to pile up. It soon became clear that one twin had often reacted to what was happening to the other, and that this nearly always seemed to be something painful, frightening or life-threatening.

For example:

• A mother is holding one of her twin babies when he suddenly goes into convulsions and screams in terror for no obvious reason. His twin is lying silently on the couch beside her, face downwards. He is turning blue and suffocating. His mother is convinced that she managed to save him only because his brother sounded the alarm. The twins are just three days old.

• A five-month-old wakes up as the clock strikes ten and startles his father by crying desperately for a quarter of an hour as if in pain, then suddenly stopping and going straight back to sleep. In a hospital several miles away his brother is having a painful injection. His mother happens to note the time – 10 p.m.

• The mother of another pair of five-month-olds notices that when one of them is having his inoculation, he takes it quite calmly – but the other one yells his head off.

- A student at a New York university wakes up suddenly at 6 a.m., certain that something has happened to her sister (in Arizona). So it has – a bomb has just gone off right outside her home.
- The sister of a woman in London who is having a painful pregnancy telephones from Australia, begging the obstetrician to operate as soon as he can. 'I can't stand the pain,' she tells him.
  (The obstetrician tells me this kind of thing is quite common with twins.)

My new file became thicker and thicker. There was the case of the Manchester man who woke up with a start, feeling as if he had just been hit on the head, and the next day learnt that at exactly the same time his twin had fallen and banged his head. There were the two brothers who went skiing on different pistes in the Alps – both fell, each breaking the same leg in the same place, again at exactly the same time. There was the little Spanish girl who suddenly developed a red blister on her hand at the time her sister, several miles away, burned her hand with an iron, causing an identical blister. There was the woman in New York who was suddenly taken ill, saying that she felt as if she was having a baby, which she certainly wasn't. Her sister in Europe was, though, several weeks prematurely.

So it went on and on. The evidence was abundant, compelling, and above all consistent. Again and again I would hear the same stories – in the case of the blue baby, two that were identical in every detail. Some of what I was hearing and reading might have involved faulty memory, misreporting, exaggeration or pure invention. But all of it? I doubted it, especially after following up some of the cases I mentioned above (and will discuss later in more detail) and talking at length to those concerned. Could anybody, I wondered, deny the fact that identical twins are telepathic, or at least that some of them are?

Apparently they could. Asked in a television programme for her views on telepathy, one twin replied indignantly, as if she had been insulted, 'Oh, get real. The possibilities of that are remote, what with all the big scientific stuff. If it was that possible a phenomenon it would have been picked up by now. So why ask this daft question?'[3]

Author Peter Watson was equally dismissive in his book on the twin research at the University of Minnesota. 'There is no evidence whatsoever,' he wrote, 'to support the idea that any form of parapsychological phenomena [which include telepathy] are involved in the twin bond.' Noting that 'very few studies have been done but the results have all been negative', he concludes that 'there is not the slightest scintilla of a suggestion that twins have some way of communicating with each other that brings on coincidence. Or, if there is, the twins know nothing of it.'[4]

As co-director of the Minnesota programme for many years, Dr Nancy Segal must have spent much of her working life in the company of twins. Yet on the subject of telepathy, also sometimes called extra-sensory perception or ESP, she makes herself very clear: 'The bottom line is that I feel there's no evidence for ESP in twins.' She does concede that 'you hear from twins that yes, they have this connection' and that 'you hear a lot about what I call "ESP-like" events', but she puts these all down to 'genetic underpinning'.[5]

One of the first British twin researchers, Dr James Shields of the Institute of Psychiatry, London, was prepared to go further, if only very slightly. 'Claims of telepathic-like experiences are so often made, and not only by the hysterically inclined, that one suspects there is more to it than simply the wish to be alike,' he wrote in 1962.[6] I cannot help wondering in passing if an experience that is 'ESP-like' or 'telepathic-like' might actually be telepathic.

How, you would be forgiven for asking, can the experts dismiss something that so many people take for granted? There are at least three answers to this question; later, I will be looking at the subject of taboo with regard to one of them. Another reason for the failure

to take the concept of telepathy seriously is that the opinions of many experts are strongly influenced by the Minnesota research, which concentrates, or did initially, mainly on twins separated at birth and reunited as adults. The aim of this research is to sort out the relative importance of genetics and upbringing – or nature and nurture – which can be of practical value to medical and psychological research. Reunited twins are ideal for this, but they are far from ideal for research into telepathy, for a very simple reason: if they are separated at birth, when they are barely conscious, they are not going to develop any kind of bond, let alone a special one. How can they, if – as has often been the case – they are not even told they have a twin until well into adulthood?

As I show throughout this book, for telepathy to take place between twins or anybody else, there usually has to be a bond of some kind. It does not take place between strangers, with rare exceptions, and since the identical twin bond is one of the closest there is, if we want to study telepathy at its strongest this is where we should look for it and expect to find the best evidence for it.

The third answer to the question above is very simple: the necessary research has not been done. Nancy Segal was making a polite understatement when she described what few studies there have been of twin telepathy (none of them at Minnesota, by the way) as 'so poor you can't even use them to make an informed judgment'. I outline just how poor some of them were in Chapter 3, which makes for rather depressing reading. I hope the rest of the book makes up for it.

There have been numerous studies of telepathy since the 1880s, yet there has never been a serious twin telepathy study on a large enough scale to enable us to make a well-informed judgment. Not one. I have included such studies as I have been able to track down in the hope that they encourage new researchers – and one of the main aims of this book is to encourage new research – to avoid others' past mistakes.

Despite its title, this book is concerned with telepathy in general as much as, if not more than, telepathy between twins. I have concentrated on the twin connection because there is much about it that does not seem to have been said before, and because I believe it provides an important clue to the mystery of *how* telepathy actually happens as well as *when*. It also shows the telepathic signal at full volume, as it were, at which not only information is transmitted at a distance but so are emotions, physical sensations and even symptoms such as burns and bruises. With rare exceptions, links of this intensity do not exist between non-twins. So you might say that the proper study of telepathy is identical twins.

Is telepathy important in this age of high-tech instant communication? I think it is for two reasons. One is that any new discovery about ourselves, however trivial or controversial it may seem, should be explored to see where it leads. The other is that if telepathy exists – and I will have failed if any reader gets to the end of this book without being satisfied that it does – it shows there must be at least one more dimension. I find that very interesting and well worth investigating.

Although the word was coined only in 1882, telepathy seems to have been around for a long time. The 16th-century philosopher Heinrich Cornelius Agrippa stated that 'it is possible for someone to convey thoughts to someone else, however far apart they may be from each other.' Paracelsus claimed that 'a person on this side of the ocean may make a person on the other side hear what is said on this side.'[7] Francis Bacon mentioned 'the binding of thoughts' early in the 17th century and even suggested ways of testing it statistically.[8]

Twins have also been around for a long time, yet it was not until the 1840s, as far as I have been able to discover (and that applies to all claims made in this book) that anybody even suggested that there might be a special link between them. This is not surprising, for before we had the kind of popular media we have today, the personal experiences of ordinary people were not generally made public, except, of course, by novelists, who need a regular supply of such raw material.

So it is not surprising that the first clear description of the special twin connection comes from a novel in which the heroes are a pair of identical twins.

CHAPTER 2
THIS COMMON ENTITY

We had to be separated with a scalpel, which means that however far apart we are now we still have one and the same body, so that whatever impression, physical or mental, one of us perceives has its after-effect on the other. Well, these last few days I have been feeling sad, morose and sombre for no reason, and suffering terrible pangs. It's clear that my brother is feeling profoundly sorrowful.

This is how one of the heroes of Alexandre Dumas's novel *The Corsican Brothers* (1844) describes how it feels to be an identical twin, in his case a conjoined or 'Siamese' one who had been successfully separated from his brother. He may be going too far in claiming that twins pick up all mental and physical impressions from each other but, as I have already pointed out, what they communicate best is bad news – depression, illness, accidents or of course death. Here is how this twin describes what happened to him one day when he was out on horseback in the Corsican countryside with a friend:

Then, just as I was putting my watch in my pocket after looking at the time, I received such a violent blow on my side that I passed out. When I opened my eyes, I was lying on the ground in the arms of Orlandini, who was splashing water in my face.
'Hey,' he said, 'what's happened to you?'
'My God,' I replied, 'I have no idea. But didn't you hear a shot?'
'No, I didn't.'

'I feel as if I had just been shot – here.' I showed him where I felt the pain.

'For a start,' Orlandini went on, 'there wasn't any kind of shot, and what's more there isn't a hole in your jacket.'

'In that case,' I replied, 'it's my brother who has just been killed.'[1]

As indeed he had been, in a duel outside Paris, some 600 miles away. His twin's reaction was so similar to that of Norris McWhirter that it seems likely that Dumas was doing what novelists often do – putting a real-life experience into a work of fiction. He is known to have visited Corsica in the early 1840s, and his novel is, I am assured by a Corsican, an accurate depiction of the landscape and social customs of the period. Its narrator, who sounds very much like Dumas himself, describes how he met the young man who told him about the fate of his twin, and it seems more probable that the author collected it at first hand than that he made it up.

Why else would he introduce such a (then) outlandish idea as twin telepathy, or indeed any kind of telepathy, into what was otherwise one of his typical tales of action and romance, unless he had been told about it by somebody who had experienced it? There was nothing in print that could have given him the idea. Moreover, Dumas was a notorious plagiarist who was quite capable of inserting whole chunks of other writers' works into his own, and I am sure he would not have hesitated to make use of a good and original story that he picked up on his travels. It is also interesting that he describes only the kind of telepathy that twins do experience – with his novelist's licence he could have invented all kinds of marvels of the mind, but he did not. He kept to the facts.

It is of course probable that he had heard about the original 'Siamese' twins Chang and Eng Bunker (who were actually Chinese, but were brought up in what was then Siam). They were touring Europe as circus freaks in the 1840s, but in all the accounts

I have read about their sad lives there is no mention of telepathy at all. So on the whole I suspect that *The Corsican Brothers* was based on a true story.

A COINCIDENCE SO STRANGE

Whether it was or not, nobody took much notice of the book, and it is mentioned in only one of 12 biographies of Dumas that I have consulted, and then only in passing, with no identification of its source. It is also worth noting that there is not a word about telepathy in George Sand's novel about twins, *La petite Fadette* (1848), in which the heroes' differences rather than their similarities are emphasized. Nor was there more than a hint of a special twin bond in a very dull book of memoirs called *The Twin Brothers* by James Dixon (1824). He recalls passing out one hot day in a cornfield, agreeing with those who would say there was nothing remarkable about that, but:

> *What will such people divine when I inform them that my brother-twin during the same afternoon when we were fifteen miles asunder was afflicted in exactly the same manner? A coincidence so strange cannot be accounted for by any common-place reasons.*

Few would agree with that opinion today. It could easily have been no more than a coincidence. Both twins could be expected to respond in the same way to the same stimulus – a combination of heat and fatigue, assuming the 'brother-twin' was also cutting corn, which the author fails to mention. This is a good example of something that might look like telepathy but could have been quite normal. Dixon's idea that the incident showed 'the finger of Providence' at work shows that the idea of a special twin connection had never occurred to him.[2]

It was quite some time before it occurred to anybody at all other than Dumas, apparently. The evidence may have been there, but hardly anybody went to look for it or to put it in print. One who did was a French country doctor named Baume, who found one of his cases so unusual that he wrote it up in some detail and sent it to one of his country's leading scientific journals.[3]

It had all begun at three o'clock one morning in 1863 when a railway worker named François woke up after a vivid dream, leaping out of bed and shouting, 'I've caught the thief!' He then started jumping up and down and dancing around the room. This was an odd way for anyone to behave, but odder still was the fact that his twin brother Martin, who lived six miles away, woke up at exactly the same time after having exactly the same dream and did the same things, rushing around and claiming to have caught the thief – the thief in question being whoever had stolen some money from a box in which both brothers kept their savings.

Later that day Martin, still in a highly agitated state, walked out of his house and threw himself in the river. Luckily, one of his sons had followed him and was able to save him from drowning. Some gendarmes then turned up and, presumably recognizing Martin as a man with a history of mental problems, took him off to the local asylum after a bit of a struggle which François happened to see from a distance. Apparently under the impression that Martin was being arrested as the thief, he went to the river and jumped in at exactly the same place as his brother. This time, there was nobody around to fish him out and he drowned. Dr Baume, who investigated this case with commendable thoroughness, makes it clear that he had not seen his brother's suicide attempt.

Martin died three days later while in Dr Baume's care. 'This,' he noted in his report, 'is how two brothers died, their madness, developed as a result of the same cause, showed roughly the same features, began at the same time and would have ended, without either's knowledge, in the same form of suicide at the same place.' Dr Baume presumably spoke to members of both men's families, for he insists that both had used exactly the same words and phrases after their identical dreams.

This case is typical of many that seem to be a mixture of the normal and the not so normal. The twins' mental states and suicidal tendencies presumably had a genetic origin, yet how about those identical dreams? Twins do have them – indeed, one pair to be mentioned in a later chapter have assured me they always have them – and it is hard to see how this can be explained by 'genetic underpinning'. The French twins' use of the same words, phrases and actions suggests that they were in some kind of contact – sharing a mind, as it were.

SURPRISE PRESENTS

Dr Baume's report seems to have encouraged other doctors to write up cases involving twins, and it seems that there was something of an epidemic of synchronized insanity around the middle of the 19th century! The distinguished British scientist Francis Galton was intrigued by these cases and they seem to have prompted him to do some original field work, almost certainly the first of its kind anywhere. He wrote letters to everybody he could think of, asking if they knew any twins and enclosing a questionnaire to be passed on to them. (The original of one of his letters is in the Science Library's special collection.) He had an encouraging response, and in 1876 he published a short article on 'The history of twins, as a criterion of the relative powers of nature and nurture', and although it was these that were his main interest he took the trouble to ask about twins' personal experiences. He found 35 cases of 'extremely close resemblance', in 11 of which there was evidence for 'similarity in the association of their ideas'. He found twins who 'make the same remarks on the same occasion' or 'begin singing the same song at the same moment'. He also saw examples of that old favourite in the twin repertoire, one finishing a sentence the other has started, which nowadays we would put down to what is known as 'thought concordance' rather than telepathy.

One of Galton's cases gave him special pause for thought. A man had been visiting Scotland, where he had decided to buy a set of engraved champagne glasses as a surprise present for his brother in England. It turned out to be more of a surprise than he had expected, because when he delivered his present he was offered a welcome-home gift by his twin – of an identical set of champagne glasses. 'Other anecdotes of like kind have reached me about these twins,' Galton adds, but unfortunately gives no details of them.[4]

I mentioned earlier that the twin telepathy message almost invariably brings bad news. Sometimes, though, it is not a specific message that is transmitted, but an impulse, as in this case, to do a certain thing at a certain time. A modern example of this is described by Gloria Vanderbilt and Thelma Furness in their joint autobiography:

> *I, Thelma, bought a birthday present for Gloria. It was a statuette of a Dresden dancing girl, and I carefully wrapped it and hid it so Gloria wouldn't know what I intended to give her. When... we exchanged our presents I was crushed to see the look of disappointment on her face when she opened the package.*

Sure enough, Gloria's present to Thelma was of an identical statuette (bought, incidentally, at a different store at a different time), and the reason she was disappointed was that she thought Thelma was giving her back her own gift, presumably not wanting it. This was one of 'innumerable' examples of 'this strange sharing of each other's thoughts and experiences... this psychic bond, this common entity which is in many ways the strongest influence in our lives – almost as if we were Siamese twins without the physical connection.'[5]

COMMON ENTITIES

To return to Galton, it is worth noting that while he went to some length to sort out the relative effects on twins of genetics (nature) and upbringing (nurture), he does not seem to have tried to separate their experiences that could be considered normal from those that could not. Indeed, the champagne glass case is the only one of its kind that he mentions. Perhaps he can be forgiven for this because in 1875, when he wrote a shorter version of his 1876 essay, telepathy was simply not discussed, at least not in polite scientific society.

It was discussed, though, in some detail in September 1876 at a meeting of the elite of the scientific establishment, the British Association for the Advancement of Science. The speaker was a young physics professor named William Barrett (later Sir William), who read a paper on 'Some phenomena associated with abnormal conditions of mind' in which he claimed that experiments of his own in mesmerism had convinced him that 'the existence of a distinct idea in my own mind gave rise to an image of the idea in the subject's mind; not always a clear image, but one that could not fail to be recognised as a more or less distorted reflection of my own thought'. In a letter to *The Times* he specifically mentioned 'the action of one mind upon another, across space, without the intervention of the senses'.[6]

He got into trouble later when it was revealed that some of his star subjects, the five Creery sisters, had been deceiving him by using signalling codes. This might have consigned the very idea of telepathy, or what Barrett called thought transference, to the scientific dustbin had it not been for the founding in 1882 of the Society for Psychical Research. Its founders wasted no time in getting down to work collecting evidence for what one of them, the poet and classical scholar Frederic Myers, called telepathy, which he defined as 'transmission of thought independently of the recognised channels of sense'.

He and his colleagues Edmund Gurney and Frank Podmore were less interested in the antics of naughty young ladies in Victorian parlours than in the spontaneous experiences of ordinary people from all walks of life, and they embarked on a vast survey involving the writing of thousands of letters asking people about their psychic experiences of all kinds, especially telepathy. The evidence poured in, much of it being followed up by letters and personal interviews, and the SPR team ended up with more than 700 cases for which they could find no normal explanation.

They also picked up the twin-link baton where Galton had dropped it. In their huge two-volume report published in 1886 they wrote (the emphasis is theirs):

On the supposition that a natural bond between two persons is a favourable condition for telepathic influence, there is one group of people among whom we might expect to find a disproportionate number of instances, namely twins.

This is just what they did find, and the five cases they considered strong enough to publish were apparently the first of their kind to appear in print anywhere. The fact that all five of them involved death or near death prompted the authors to make what now seems the obvious point that twin 'coincidences' fall into two categories: the predictable and the unpredictable. In the first, it was as if two identical watches had been wound up together, set to the same time and left to tick until they stopped. If one of them went fast or slow, the other could be expected to do the same. In the case of twins (by which I mean identical ones throughout this book unless otherwise indicated), if one had a disease with an internal (genetic) cause, the other could be expected to get it as well. It might seem like an amazing coincidence but it would be quite normal and indeed predictable.

Some coincidences, however, were not predictable. Myers and his colleagues referred to Galton's champagne glass case as one of those that 'seem outside the range of a pre-established physiological harmony', as were the five cases they published. One of these involved the Rev. J. M. Wilson, a well known mathematician who was headmaster of Clifton College. He recalled:

I was at Cambridge... in full health, boating, football and the like, and by no means subject to hallucinations or morbid fancies. One evening I felt extremely ill, trembling, with no apparent cause whatever; nor did it seem to me at the time to be a physical illness, a chill of any kind. I was frightened, I was totally unable to overcome it. I remember a sort of struggle with myself, resolving that I would go on with my mathematics, but it was in vain. I became convinced that I was dying... It was a sort of panic fear, the chill of approaching death that was on me.

He had never felt anything like this before, and the impression was so strong that he went to a friend's room and stayed there for about three hours. He then calmed down and went back to his room, and the following morning felt perfectly well, but:

In the afternoon came a letter to say that my twin brother had died the evening before in Lincolnshire. I am quite clear of the fact that I never once thought of him, nor was his presence with me even dimly imagined. He had long been ill of consumption, but I had not heard from him for some days, and there was nothing to make me think his death was near. It took me altogether by surprise.

This is a particularly clear case in which emotions rather than thoughts were picked up. In fact, Rev. Wilson emphasized that he had not thought of his brother and even feared it was he himself who was dying. This confusion of identity between twins, which turned up in another of the SPR cases, supports the view held by many twins that they are indeed a 'common entity', as Gloria Vanderbilt and Thelma Furness put it.

James Carroll, one of a pair of twins in their thirties, had every reason to feel cheerful one morning in 1878 when he suddenly felt 'a strange sadness and depression' come over him for no obvious reason. Unlike Rev. Wilson, he did think of his brother and promptly sat down to write a letter to him. He also experienced some identity confusion, though, since he remembered saying out loud 'My brother or I will break down.'

The following week he suffered another sudden and severe depression, which was interrupted by the arrival of a telegram with the news that his brother was seriously ill and wanted him to come at once. The brother died two days later, and James Carroll learned that he had been speaking about him 'in great distress' at the time of his second attack of depression – the first one coinciding with the first day of the fatal illness. Just before the telegram arrived, he had again felt that 'something might suddenly happen to me' rather than to his twin.

In another case provided by a clergyman, it was again an emergency signal, a clearer one this time, that was transmitted. One day when his twin was away on a long sailing holiday, Rev. A. J. Maclean suddenly 'felt certain there was something wrong with my brother'. He made a note of the time, something we researchers only wish everybody would always do! In this case the twin at sea also produced written evidence in the form of his diary. 'On the day in question,' his brother told the SPR team, 'they had encountered a storm, in which all the masts were injured and things washed away. They gave up all for lost.' They were, however, able to reach land safely.

An even more vivid signal was picked up by Mrs Storie in a dream in which she seemed to see, in great detail, the death of her non-identical twin brother in Australia. She saw him lying beside a railway line, and behind him was an engine with a curiously shaped funnel of a kind she had never seen before. She also saw a clergyman named Johnstone sitting in the train, as she noted in the long account of the dream she wrote about a week later, after she had learned that her brother had indeed been killed by a train. Myers and co. investigated this case exceptionally thoroughly, perhaps feeling that it was too good to be true, but were satisfied that Mrs Storie was telling the truth. They discovered that engines in the part of Australia where her brother had died did have funnels of the kind she had described, also that Rev Johnstone had been on board. The woman's husband, another clergyman, testified that his wife did have the dream on the day she said she did.

A lifelike apparition was also a feature of the last of the SPR cases. It was so lifelike, in fact, that the witness, Mr Evans, thought he really had seen his brother looking up at him from the pit of a theatre in Toronto, where he was on a visit. He was staring at him 'in an intent, weird and agonising manner that caused a feeling of awe to overpower me. as I recognised the features of my own twin brother, who at that time was in China.'

He was indeed in China, and on the evening in question he was dying.

SUBTLE AFFINITIES

The SPR founders, in an amazingly short space of time, collected more evidence for telepathy than had ever been gathered before, and they were the first to realize that there was something special about twin telepathy.[7] They described their survey confidently as 'the foundation stone of a study which will loom large in the approaching era' as indeed it did as far as telepathy in general was concerned, and it still looms large today as an example of how much original evidence can be found by those who go out into the field and look for it instead of waiting for it to turn up at their laboratories.

As far as twin telepathy research was concerned, however, the foundation stone was not to be built on for more than 50 years. Even then, building work stopped almost as soon as it started, to be followed by several more stops and starts that went on until late in the 20th century, by the end of which the whole building site seemed to have been abandoned.

The first of these starts seemed promising, because it was made by an eminent academic, Professor Horatio H. Newman, head of the zoology department at the University of Chicago and author of the first major study of twinhood in all its aspects. He was well qualified to study the subject since he himself was a twin. In 1942 he published a book called *Twins and Super-Twins* in which he included a section on telepathy, giving several examples from his own experience of what looked very much like it.

He happened to have a pair of identical (or 'one-egg', as he called them) twins among his graduate students, and he did what few other researchers seem to have done – asked some twins themselves if they had any experience of telepathy. His pair were 'hard-boiled, critical biologists' who had been taught that 'the naturalistic explanation of biological phenomena is the only orthodox one' and that 'nothing is accepted as fact unless it has been experimentally proved'. Their replies surprised him.

They both believed that there was 'some subtle affinity between one-egg twins that makes it possible for one to know what the other is thinking about. They themselves have almost daily experiences that support the view that they are in communication without employing the ordinary media of exchange in common use.' Their connection, they added, was as much of a mystery to them as it was to everybody else.

Newman came across one or two cases that must have surprised even him. A young woman told him how she and her sister had revised for an exam, or rather failed to do so. They had left their revision a little late, so they decided to read half the set books each.

On the examination, the main question dealt with materials that our informant claims to have neither read nor discussed with her sister. When she began to think about the matter, however, the answer came to her and she wrote it without difficulty. The answer was so much like that written by her twin sister that the teacher suspected copying and called them in for an explanation.[8]

They managed to stay out of trouble by pointing out that they had been sitting too far apart to be able to communicate with each other in any way – well, any normal way. I have several similar cases of simultaneous exam-writing, one of them dating from the First World War in which two twins, generals Felix and Theodore Brett, aroused so much suspicion after turning in identical exam papers that Allied commander Marshal Joffre personally ordered an official enquiry, at which the twins were found innocent of any wrongdoing. Yet the most unusual case of this kind comes from Newman's collection. A pair of twin boys had a highly sceptical teacher who had become so suspicious of some kind of trickery, because they kept on writing identical exam papers, that he had them take their Latin paper in different rooms. That, he thought, would do the trick, but it didn't.

> On the day of the examination Joe's twin was given the questions in the teacher's office but seemed unable to begin.
> 'Why don't you get to work?' inquired the teacher impatiently.
> 'I am not ready,' responded Joe's twin, somewhat sulkily.
> After another long period the teacher, noting that the boy was still idling, said crossly, 'Why don't you get to work? Your brother will be through before you get started.'

The boy still refused to get started. At that point the head teacher came in and said there had been a mix-up. Joe had been sitting in his room for half an hour without being given his paper. When this finally was given to him, both twins – in their separate rooms and heavily supervised – immediately set to work, finished at the same time and went back into the main classroom together. Later, the headmaster summoned them to his office.

> 'Boys,' he exclaimed, 'your Latin papers are identical. The same words, the same syntax, the same grammar but, strangest of all, the same mistakes. But of one thing I am sure, you did not cheat. It must be because you are twins.'

Professor Newman gives a good example of the kind of explaining-away favoured by scientists of his day. A sceptical colleague pointed out that what he called 'the appearance' of telepathy was simply the consequence of identical twins having the same brains and nervous systems. Dr Segal was making a similar claim 40 years later for a solely genetic explanation. Yet if this were true, we could expect twins always to do exactly the same things all the time, which they do not.

The sceptic used the analogy of identical watches to make his point, as the SPR researchers had done, and we can take this analogy further. Suppose we take our two watches to different places and then smash one of them with a hammer. We would not expect the other one to fall to pieces at the same time. Yet this is, in effect, just what twins do, which is why investigating them is so important. No other people show community of sensation at a distance on anything like the scale that they do.

Newman ended his brief survey of twin telepathy with a direct appeal to Dr J. B. Rhine, the founder in the early Thirties of academic psychical research, now known as parapsychology, at Duke University in Durham, North Carolina:

> *Since so many pairs of one-egg twins seem to have more than ordinary powers of intercommunication, I should like to suggest to Dr Rhine and his associates... that they try out their telepathic or extra-sensory perception technique upon some pairs of one-egg twins who claim to have these unusual capacities. Such a series of experiments would, in my opinion, go far toward either confirming Dr Rhine's theories or wiping the whole highly controversial question of telepathy off the scientific shelf.*

ENTER AND EXIT J. B. RHINE

This was quite a reasonable suggestion, and it is hard to imagine how any professional parapsychologist could fail to show interest in the kind of evidence Newman had published. Rhine, however, did not show very much. More than 20 years after Newman's book was published, another one came out with the same title, covering much the same ground and taking a similar if more cautious approach to telepathy. Its author, Dr Amram Scheinfeld, at least admitted it to be a possibility, and went a step further than Newman by approaching Rhine directly, reckoning that if anybody knew anything about twin telepathy, he would.[9]

Rhine's reply was not encouraging. 'Although popular belief would have led us to expect that there was exceptional telepathic communication between identical twins, nothing outstanding has occurred in any single case of identical twins tested so far.' (He seems to have overlooked the fact that Newman's opinions were based not on popular belief but on first-hand evidence.) He added that although he had heard accounts of 'what would appear to be exceptional telepathic rapport between identical twins', he did not think they were any different from similar accounts involving any closely related pairs or friends.

Scheinfeld could be forgiven for assuming that Rhine had been studying dozens of twins for 30 years and was giving an opinion based on a mass of data. Yet he wasn't. A search through every issue of the *Journal of Parapsychology*, in which Rhine's experimental results had been published since it was founded in 1937 reveals the grand total of papers on twin telepathy research to be three.[10]

The first, published in the same year, was by a graduate student at Fordham University, and it sounds like one of those Dr Segal described as 'so poor you can't even to use them to make an informed judgment'. Under the pretentious and misleading title 'An experimental investigation of the telepathy phenomenon in twins', it was introduced in an editorial (by Rhine) as 'an important research project' into 'an oft-suggested phenomenon... of widespread interest'. Yet only six pairs of twins were studied, of which just one was of identicals. Results were at chance level, and the whole thing was a complete waste of time. Its only point of interest is the fact that the author did not cite a single reference, suggesting that this was the first so-called experimental investigation of its kind.

It probably caused lasting damage to serious twin research by giving the false impression that the twin connection had been proved not to exist. 'Ah,' we can hear the parapsychology community sighing with relief, 'now that's out of the way we can get on with something else.'

The second study, in 1946, was slightly more useful, showing that closely related pairs were better than unrelated ones at drawing pictures of what their experimental partners in another room were thinking about. This was not specifically a study of twins but of close pairs in general, and again only one pair of identicals was used. However, it seems to have been quite carefully done and the results do support my claim that the closer the bond, the clearer the evidence for telepathy.

As far as Rhine's involvement in twin research is concerned, that's about it apart from an eight-line note published in 1960 describing an experiment in which six pairs of identicals had been tested (not stated how or for what) and shown overall nonsignificant results although one pair scored well above chance level. It seems, then, that by 1960 the total number of pairs of identical twins who had been tested for telepathy in Rhine's laboratory was just eight. Not, some might think, a large enough sample from which to draw any conclusions at all, except that Rhine did not do the kind of research he should have done which is to test twins for what they do best. In Rhine's heyday, the Thirties to the Sixties, more or less, parapsychology was determined to be accepted as a respectable field of science, and to win that respect and overcome the taboo against anything that could be called psychic or paranormal, it had to be seen to be using the methodology of conventional science. This approach paid off, with the Parapsychological Association (of professional workers in the field) finally being affiliated to the American Association for the

Advancement of Science in 1969. However, the new approach tended to make researchers more interested in statistics than in real life.

Rhine's subjects were usually forced to spend hours and hours guessing which of the five Zener cards (star, cross, square, circle or wavy lines) somebody was looking at on the other side of the screen. Basil Shackleton, who took part in a series of British experiments that were meant to repeat Rhine's work, once memorably pounded the table at a lecture he gave to the SPR, bellowing 'I was bored, bored, BORED!'

Commenting on research of this kind, Mary Rosambeau, author of an important twin survey to be mentioned later, notes drily that 'studies like these can prove that this is not the sort of extrasensory perception which twins experience. They do not disprove that they feel anything at all.'[11] Precisely.

A good way to demonstrate what twins do experience would be to separate a pair of twins and then give one of them a whack on the head with a saucepan. The distant twin would be more likely to react, I would predict, than a control non-twin. This is what is known as a thought experiment, one that you do not actually do but imagine doing in order to make a point. Luckily, as it happens, I do not have to do this experiment because several unfortunate twins have already done it for me.

One of them is a Manchester taxi driver who happened to mention a strange experience he had just had to one of his passengers, author David Lorimer. He had gone to bed early but had been rudely awakened at 11 p.m. feeling as if he had just been hit on the head although he had not been. The following day he phoned his brother and learned what he had been doing at eleven o'clock the night before. The answer – falling downstairs and banging himself on the head.[12]

'There seems to be a human connection that needs explaining,' Lorimer comments. There does indeed, and attempts to explain it have been very slow in coming. Despite Rhine's failure to do any useful twin research apart from that single 1946 experiment, his methods continued to be used by other parapsychologists with not very exciting results, as I show in the next chapter. I include their work, inadequate though much of it was, because there is something useful to be learned from it. As Kepler wrote in his *Tertius Interveniens* (1610), if a 'diligent hen' pecks and pokes around long enough in the 'rotting dunghill' she will find the occasional pearl or even gold,[13] and as we start to peck our way through the twin research literature from 1961 onwards, we strike gold straight away.

CHAPTER 3
AN INTERESTING HYPOTHESIS

'We need techniques for selecting suitable subjects for ESP experiments. We have to be able to work under conditions that give the phenomena we study every opportunity to emerge. There is little point in... testing a new drug for virus pneumonia on tuberculous patients.' This is how a Toronto-based team of psychologists – Robert Sommer, Humphry Osmond (better known for his LSD research) and Lucille Pancyr – began their 1961 report on their preparations for a large-scale twin telepathy experiment.[1] Although, apparently for reasons beyond their control, they never got around to doing the actual experiment (and nor has anyone else as yet), this report on their preliminary work contains a whole string of pearls.

They chose twins because they were well aware of the need for a close emotional bond for a successful telepathy experiment, and other closely bonded groups such as parents and young children (or, I might add, pets and their owners), are less suitable for testing although, as I will show, they can still provide good evidence for spontaneous telepathy. The Toronto team found a total of 35 twins, 14 pairs and seven single ones and began by asking them – as Newman had done 20 years previously with his twin students – to describe any 'ESP-like' experiences that they had had.

Twelve of them believed that they could communicate with their brother or sister by telepathy, and several were convinced that they already had done so. For example:

Yes, I felt that I could communicate thoughts... When my

twin was about to do something he shouldn't, I could communicate by thoughts rather than tell him directly.

I can communicate ideas with a minimum of explanation. I can also tell how my twin was feeling even when my father couldn't.

We both think the same things at the same time and I can tell what her feelings are.

I always know her mood without talking to her or even seeing her.

When my twin goes out, I can imagine what he is doing and see the place, like right now, even if I've never been there or seen the place described.

One twin mentioned an incident that, at the time she was questioned, had only just taken place. 'This afternoon, when I was going to ask her for some money, she asked me if I wanted some. She seemed to know.' Another observed that she and her sister were constantly buying identical gifts for the same person although they lived in different cities.

Even more interesting were twins' reports of actual physical sensations being received. One recalled how she had felt pain when her sister cut her hand and when she had burned herself. Three seemed to have felt exactly what Dumas's Corsican brother had felt when his twin was in trouble ('sad, morose and sombre for no reason').

I frequently know when there's something wrong, not specifically though. I just feel on edge and unhappy for no reason.

Once when Carol was in Saskatoon and I was in Vancouver,

*I had the vague feeling that something was wrong... Carol...
was ill, although not seriously.*

*Once I felt rather blue and depressed without knowing why.
My twin phoned from Ontario then because of some
difficulty...*

Already, clear categories are beginning to emerge showing the
kinds of ways in which twins experience telepathy or community
of sensation, lending support to Galton's original finding that only
about one third of identicals have a special closeness. This finding
has stood the test of time, all the surveys I have yet seen putting
the percentage of telepathy-proneness among identicals at between
30 and 40.

The Toronto team missed what look like some good
opportunities. Why, for instance, did they not ask the fellow who
could see where his brother was 'right now' where he was and what
he was doing? They deserve credit, though, for identifying the kind
of twins that were most likely to experience telepathy. They had to
be absolutely identical, preferably to the extent of thinking of
themselves as one person, as some do. They had to be open to the
idea of telepathy even if they had never experienced it, and they
had to be good at visualizing, since there seemed to be a link
beween ESP and imagery. (It is now well established that creative
people such as artists and musicians are much better than others at
telepathy tests.)

'Our inquiry,' the Toronto team concluded in their report, the
first addition of any value to that foundation stone laid in 1886,
'suggests that twins are a class of people who are predisposed to
having ESP and with whom little work, and none of that
systematic, has been attempted.' That was written in 1961, and the
position was much the same 40 years later, long after many another
promising start had ground to a halt.

A Front-Page Story

In 1965, when there was no sign of anybody following up the Toronto work, the subject of twin telepathy suddenly became front-page news after a short article had appeared in the leading American scientific journal *Science* under the mysterious title 'Extrasensory electroencephalographic induction between identical twins'.[2] Its authors, Philadelphia ophthalmologists T. D. Duane and Thomas Behrendt, claimed that two pairs of identical twins had shown that when alpha brain rhythm (that's about 7 to 13 cycles per second) was artificially induced in one of each pair of young men in their twenties, the brainwave chart of the other one showed that his brain also went into alpha rhythm at exactly the same time. Had telepathy, which is what this amounts to, been proved to exist at last and actually recorded on a chart? To judge from the illustration printed with the report, it certainly looked as if it had.

Yet there were problems. A further 13 pairs of twins tested did not show the same effect, and letters began to pour in from readers of *Science* complaining of just about everything to do with the article. The sample was too small, the researchers had not said how long the test period had lasted, how many control pairs of non-twins were tested, or what proportion of the stimuli produced an induction effect. Duane and Behrendt said they had repeated the successful tests 'several times', but one irate reader wanted to know 'how many replications is "several" and how many opportunities were provided for the effect to show itself or fail to appear?' Parapsychologist Charles Tart reckoned that the article 'would have been rejected on first reading by all of the four reputable parapsychological journals'.[3]

The authors made a rather half-hearted attempt to defend themselves, which served only to discredit them still further. They admitted that their methods had not been perfect, but still insisted that 'our previous research led us to the proposal of an interesting hypothesis. Preliminary experimentation has indicated that we may be on the right track.' There were, they said, at least a million twins in America and no shortage of well-equipped laboratories. Any qualified researcher could easily repeat their experiment, so why didn't they?

Admitting that 'only hard, quantitatively acceptable results will prove or refute the hypothesis', they added that 'we intend to seek such data, and it is our hope that others will do likewise.' Nobody did for some time, and Duane and Behrendt seem to have left the field of parapsychology after a very short stay, with their tails between their legs.

Yet this is not quite the end of this particular story. In 1997, *New Yorker* magazine staff writer Lawrence Wright revealed that the brainwave experiment was not funded by the National Institutes of Health as stated in the original article, but by the CIA (perhaps using the NIH as a cover).[4] Not only that, but for unfathomable reasons the paper had been classified and Wright, unaware that the anonymous CIA report he eventually obtained was the same one that had been published in *Science* for all to read, had to spend a whole year going through the rigmarole of the Freedom of Information Act to get hold of a copy.

Now why on earth would the CIA be interested in studying the brainwaves of twins? Lawrence Wright suspects it thought that if twins really could demonstrate telepathy to order, they would make good spies. There is another possibility: when authors Lynn Schroeder and Sheila Ostrander were in Bulgaria collecting material for their best-seller on psychical research in the communist countries, they learned that one of the projects under way at the Institute of Suggestology and Parapsychology in Sofia (there really is such a place – I have been there) was checking out reports of an experiment that sounds exactly like the one printed in *Science*.[5]

In the 1960s the CIA was well into its notorious MKULTRA programme, which covered every imaginable form of mind control, and at least one of its sub-projects (No. 136) is known to have involved research into ESP. At the same time, the agency was heavily involved in the disinformation business, the purpose of which is to make the enemy think you have made all kinds of discoveries that you really haven't and waste time trying to replicate them. The classic case of this was the leak of a story to the French magazine *Science et Vie* in February 1960 in which it was claimed that a US Navy submarine had been involved in ship-to-shore telepathy experiments from somewhere under the North Pole. There is no evidence that anything of the kind took place, yet the Soviets seem to have fallen for the story. Was the twin brainwave story another disinformation caper, one wonders? Could it be that the experiment was never actually done? I leave it to the conspiracy theorists to solve this minor but rather intriguing mystery.

SOME OBVIOUS REACTIONS

Duane and Behrendt's experiment, for all its faults, did serve to wake up a few members of the research community and inspire attempts to repeat it, (and as we shall see in Chapter 10 they may have had the last laugh after all). For a short time there was activity again on the building site, and in 1967 Dr Aristide Esser and colleagues at Rockland State Hospital announced that 'in a physically isolated subject, we have observed physiological reactions at the precise moment at which another person... was actively stimulated.'[6] This is exactly what Duane and Behrendt claimed to have observed.

Esser's team measured blood volume rather than brainwaves, using a device called a plethysmograph. They used 12 volunteers including (again!) just one pair of identical twins, the others being closely related or attached couples, and showed one of each pair a series of slides containing words or phrases that were either neutral, such as 'water is wet' or emotive, for example 'men are better than women'.

None of the non-twins did particularly well, perhaps because it sounds as if the experiment was very boring. In the case of the twins, however, the authors printed the complete chart record 'to show how obvious the plethysmographic reactions are'. They do indeed look obvious, but again critics could rightly complain that this result was based on a very small sample, and needed replication on a much larger scale.

In 1968 it seemed that somebody was going to do just that at long last, nearly a hundred years after Galton had noticed the 'similarity in the association of their ideas' between some twins. Frank Barron of the University of California at Berkeley got off to a flying start, sending out 435 letters to twins and getting 168 replies.[7] He weeded out the non-identicals, and was eventually able to test 26 pairs of identicals, the largest number of any twin telepathy experiment on record before or since then.

The twins were put in separate rooms and one was shown a film that had 'pronounced arousal value' while the other was hooked up to a polygraph that recorded skin resistance, heartbeat and respiration rate. The idea was to see if the monitored twin would react in any way to what the other was seeing. It was a well-thought-out experiment designed to show what twins do best, namely pick up strong emotional stimuli, and should have settled once and for all the question of whether they can really do this.

But it didn't. Only one pair showed any positive results, one of them showing a reaction to three out of eight 'arousal points' in the film. Another twin mentioned feeling 'very troubled' during her session because she was sure her sister was seeing something that frightened her, as evidently she was. However, she did not react in any measurable way.

Barron had originally planned to run a second series of experiments comparing the results of the top five and bottom five performers, but did not do so for two reasons. For a start there was only one top performer, and then there was 'an unusual amount of resistance' (it is not stated to what) from the young male volunteers who seemed to have walked out *en bloc* before they could be tested again. Something had gone badly wrong, as Barron candidly

admitted in this graphic description of how not to study twin telepathy, or indeed anything else:

> *In retrospect, the experimenter is convinced that the experimental situation itself would be unfavourable to creativity. Most of the subjects were apprehensive to start with, and certainly none got into the sort of mood that facilitates intuition, a wealth of imagery, and relaxation of ego controls. The setting was decidedly 'laboratory', the time schedule was often necessarily precise, the subjects and experimenter were not well known to one another and had little time to get acquainted, and so on.*

Sheep and Goats

Much less attention was paid in 1968 than it is today to what is known as the experimenter effect, by which the results of any experiment can be influenced in all kinds of ways by the treatment given to participants. Some of these are obvious – if volunteers, who are getting paid little, if anything, are made to perform in a cold 'laboratory' atmosphere in front of an equally cold experimenter to whom they are just numbers on the clipboard and not human beings, they are not going to do very well. If they are treated as colleagues rather than guinea pigs they are very likely to do much better.

There is another more subtle kind of experimenter effect, whereby experiments are influenced not only by scientists' behaviour and personality, but by their belief systems. This leads to a Catch-22 situation in which scientists who may seem genuinely interested in finding out if something like telepathy really exists, but are personally fairly certain that it doesn't, are going to do experiments that confirm their prejudices, to the delight of the sceptical establishment. On the other hand, those who are already convinced that telepathy exists because they have experienced it themselves are likely to get results that support their belief. It is not a case of 'I'll believe it when I see it', but of 'I'll see it when I believe it.'

This is known in the trade as the Sheep–Goat effect, and it has been repeatedly tested successfully and shown to apply to experimenters as well as subjects. It was first proposed as early as 1943 by New York psychologist Gertrude Schmeidler. She predicted that those who either accept the idea of ESP, or are at least open to the idea of it – the 'sheep' – will do better at such tests than those who reject it – the 'goats'.[8] (Today, ESP is generally referred to as 'psi', a term taken from the first letter of the Greek word for mind or soul, which parapsychologists now use to denote any kind of 'psychic' phenomenon.)

Now, much of the research I have mentioned so far has a distinctly goatish feel to it, and the problem is that negative results, however poorly done the experiments that produced them, will condition other researchers to expect more negative results – which, experimenter effects being what they are, they will probably get. In view of this, it is surprising that anybody bothered to do any more twin-psi work after 1968, when it seemed to have been proved that there was really nothing to look for.

Sceptics watching Britain's Independent Television on 17 January of that year might have concluded that the experiment shown on *The Frost Programme* was the final nail in the twin-link coffin.[9] For this, 85 pairs were separated and seated in two groups with a curtain drawn between them so that viewers could see both groups but one could not see the other. Host David Frost (now Sir David) then held up a playing card, the seven of diamonds, so that only one twin group plus the viewers could see it. Those in the second group were given full packs of playing cards and asked to hold up the card they thought their twin was trying to transmit to them.

By chance alone, 1.6 people should have got it right, and rounding that figure up to the nearest whole number gives two, which is exactly what the result was. A second experiment involved a slightly modified set of Zener cards, one of which was shown to the members of group 2 to be 'sent' through the curtain to the group 1 twins. Nineteen of the group 1 twins picked up nothing at all, and the remaining 66 chose as follows:

Wavy lines 23	Parallel lines 8
Square 16	Triangle 6
Circle 13	

By chance, 13 people should have guessed the right symbol, so the wavy lines seemed to be the clear winner, with huge odds against chance. However, it was not the card that had been used, which was the square! So these particular twins did not do very well, as I would have predicted. For a start, I would expect only 25 to 30 pairs in a group of 85 pairs of twins to have any psi ability at all, and I would not expect them to be better at card guessing than anybody else. I would also not expect ordinary people to be able to demonstrate a subtle, semiconscious effect like telepathy in a TV studio, although there has been at least one very successful live TV twin experiment, which I will describe later, but it was the exception rather than the rule. (I would say that though, wouldn't I? It was my idea!)

I would, however, expect people to be far more telepathy-prone if their conscious minds are out of the way, as when they are asleep. In a classic series of experiments, Dr Stanley Krippner and colleagues at the Maimonides Medical Center in New York spent many sleepless nights demonstrating that telepathic messages can indeed be picked up during sleep.[10]

Two of their volunteer subjects happened to be identical twins, and although they took part in only one experiment (also in 1968), it was a very successful one. The more dominant of the pair was asked to act as sender, which involved staying up all night and concentrating on a randomly selected picture every time monitoring equipment indicated that his twin, asleep in another room, was beginning a dream.

The picture on this occasion was of an Anglican church, and the twins, who were from India, happened to be Zoroastrians. The sleeper did not dream of anything resembling a Christian church in appearance, but he did recall a whole series of symbols and images related to ceremonies of his own religion, and practically nothing else. An independent judge, shown the dream transcripts and a set of six pictures, was asked which was most likely to have been the target and correctly chose the one of the church.

THOUGHT CONCORDANCE

After 1968, it seemed that the search for the twin connection was over, the building site abandoned once again apart from a couple of unconvincing attempts to add to that lonely foundation stone. In 1973, for example, Gary A. France of Illinois State University tested 16 pairs of twins (nine of them identical) together with ten pairs of siblings.[11] He was looking for 'hereditary possibilities in ESP ability', and was mainly interested in finding out if identical twins would tend to make identical guesses in Zener card tests, as researchers Carroll B. Nash and D. T. Buzby had claimed in a 1965 study.

They would indeed, and this was seen as evidence for what psychologists call TC (thought concordance) rather than for ESP. In a further experiment along similar lines at the University of Bristol published in 1993, psychologist Susan Blackmore tested 12 pairs of volunteers (three each of identical and non-identical twins and six of siblings), for both TC and ESP.[12] To simplify somewhat, in testing for TC you ask your subject to draw a picture of whatever comes to mind and then ask the other member of the pair in another room to do the same. The idea is that since identical twins tend to think concordantly (alike) they will come up with similar drawings, as one pair did very successfully, although only on one of four tests.

Testing for ESP, or psi, involves telling a subject what to draw and seeing if the other one picks it up. What Dr Blackmore found was that twins did show more concordance than the non-twin siblings, but no more aptitude for psi. Then, commenting that 'the numbers of subjects used here are too small for any firm conclusions to be drawn', she proceeded to draw one, explaining that it was all too easy to misinterpret TC as telepathy, as for instance when twins telephone each other simultaneously, say the same thing at the same time, or both start humming the same tune. 'If twins have greater thought concordance than others then they are likely to have these experiences more often,' she explained. 'This is turn may encourage them to think they have experienced the paranormal or have psychic ability whether they do or not.'

As she cheerfully admits, 'this experiment suffers from several shortcomings, including the small number of subjects and use of only one experimenter.' The fact that the tests were held in a school classroom probably did not help, as most of the volunteers were of school age. A more serious shortcoming was that although there are two references to the Toronto study I mentioned earlier, there is no mention of whether subjects were selected according to its recommendations. An experimenter hoping for a negative result could not have designed a better experiment.

Dr Blackmore, who is well known to her colleagues as an extreme sceptic, was also guilty of what looks suspiciously like bias, or at the very least some drastic spin-doctoring in her claim that Aristide Esser's experiment, described earlier, 'did not provide evidence of simultaneous responses in twins'. Evidently she missed that chart illustration and Esser's comment that it showed 'how obvious the plethysmographic reactions are'.

A very different approach was taken by Edward A. Charlesworth of the University of Houston, who went out of his way to create what he hoped would be an ideal setting for telepathy, using 20 each of identical twins, non-identical ones and non-twins as subjects.[13] They were made comfortable and played a tape in which they were told to have an imaginary dream during which the other member of the pair would look at a picture of something one would not expect to come across in the dream landscape described on the tape. Afterwards, the dreamers were shown a set of six pictures and asked to rate them as most or least likely to have been beamed at them. A rating was considered a hit if the correct picture was put in first, second or third place.

Results were baffling. Whereas guesswork would have produced 10 hits out of 20, the identical group scored only seven. The non-identicals, on the other hand, scored 15, more than twice as many. What can this mean? Are non-identicals more telepathic than identicals?

No, they aren't, although fraternal (non-identical) twins do experience telepathy, as do non-twins, as I will show in chapters 6 and 9. What Charlesworth did show, once again using a fairly small sample, was that it was the personality of the subject rather than the degree of identicality that seemed to matter, extraverts scoring much better than the introverts. This was an important addition to the spade-work done by the Toronto team in their effort to look for the ideal psi-prone subject. The way to get a good result, it seemed, was to use a pair of highly extravert identical twins, and to end this rather gloomy chapter on a positive note, I am glad to report that at least one researcher did just that with extraordinary results. These were published in a rather obscure French magazine, and this is probably the first account of them to appear in English.

TELEPATHY AND EUPHORIA

Early in the 1980s a French Red Cross doctor named Fabrice-Henri Robichon was reading up on the work of J. B. Rhine when it occurred to him that not enough research had been done into twin telepathy. So he decided to do something about that, and managed to find a pair of 20-year-old male students who were willing to be tested – apparently for his own benefit and in his spare time.[14] His may have been the first experiment of its kind

48

ever carried out in France, because he gives no references to any previous French experiments in his 1989 report. Indeed, he does not mention any researcher other than Rhine, which is probably why he decided to use the famous Zener cards for his tests.

He made up a set in which the five symbols were of different colours: blue wavy lines, green stars, black squares, yellow circles, and of course red crosses. This made the cards more interesting than the usual all-black sets and may have had a positive effect on the results, which are some of the most remarkable ever published. Robichon himself agrees that they are 'astonishing' and quotes American statistician Burton H. Camp's famous 1937 comment that 'if the Rhine investigation is to be fairly attacked, it must be on other than mathematical grounds.'

Luckily, Dr Robichon thought of giving his subjects a personality questionnaire, and found that not only were their scores almost identical, but they were both definitely extraverts. However, his tests got off to a shaky start. He decided to use three different experimental conditions for his first series of four runs through the pack. In the first, the twins could see each other over a low curtain, which of course gave them the chance to cheat by signalling at each other. Yet if they were doing this, they were not very good at it because results were very close to chance. In his report, Robichon mentions the possibility of cheating, and he may have deliberately started with lax conditions to see if they would get up to any tricks.

For the second series the twins were separated so as to exclude signalling, and the twin acting as receiver was given a set of the five symbols to look at. This, he said, would help him recognize which one 'came to mind'. It certainly seems to have, for scores shot up to 64, 92, 72, 80 and 88 per cent – chance-guessing level being only 20 per cent. Results of this order had hardly ever been reported before. The second run, in which the score was 23 out of 25 correct identifications, was done on a day when the brothers had stopped at a bar on the way and turned up 'dans un état euphorique d'ébriété sommaire' (i.e. plastered). 'It is quite reasonable to suppose,' Robichon noted,' that a brain fogged by the vapours of alcohol becomes less selective with regard to external information whether sensory or extrasensory.'

For the final series, conditions were as above except that the receiver had no set of cards to look at. Only one run was held, in which he scored 19 out of 25, or 76 per cent. One of the twins (but, the doctor noted, not the other) then developed a skin rash and the tests had to be halted. Before they could be resumed, the young men were called up for military service and Robichon lost touch with them.

An interesting feature of this series of experiments was the method of selecting target cards. Normally the pack is shuffled and the sender asked to look through the pack from top to bottom, thus looking at each card only once. Here, the sender was given a shuffled pack and asked to pick any card he liked, look at it, then put it back in the pack and shuffle again, and so on until he had looked at 25 cards. Dubious researchers, who find it hard to believe these results, have suggested to me that this invalidated the whole experiment, yet it can be argued that it made the results all the more impressive, since the receiver had no idea how many cards of each symbol would be viewed.

Extraordinary claims require extraordinarily good evidence, and Robichon's is not perfect. An independent witness would have been helpful, as would a videotape. I would also like to have known something about the men's previous telepathic exchanges, if any. Yet there is much to be learned here. Results are likely to be better if the experimenters are genuinely curious, let their subjects feel at home and enjoy themselves, and do not get upset when they arrive 'in a euphoric state of summary intoxication'. Dr Robichon also deserves credit for producing a much longer and more detailed report than most of his predecessors.

This, readers may be relieved to learn, concludes my survey of every twin telepathy experiment published in the parapsychological literature up to the end of the 20th century, with the exception of one or two that were merely repetitions of unsuccessful studies.

From the evidence presented here, there seem to be three possible conclusions:

1. Twins, identical or not, are no more telepathic than anyone else (assuming that anybody is). They may think they are because they keep experiencing coincidences, or rather concordances, which is quite natural in view of their genetic similarity.
2. Some identicals are highly psi-prone, but only about 30 per cent of them, and then normally only under certain very specific conditions such as when there is a crisis of some kind, although a small percentage may be exceptionally gifted, as the French twins seem to have been.
3. Researchers have been doing the wrong kind of experiments. They have expected telepathy to come along on cue, which is not how it happens in real life. Some have even set up experiments that seem deliberately designed to obtain negative results and put others off the idea of doing further experiments.

My money is on conclusions 2 and 3.

Now, at last, it is time to wish researchers a collective 'could do better' and head out into the real world, where there is plenty of evidence for the twin connection to be found by those who take the trouble to look for it.

CHAPTER 4

BECAUSE WE'RE TWINS

The village of Murillo de Río Leza, 10 miles from the northern Spanish town of Logroño, may seem an unlikely setting for the experiment that provided the best evidence to date for the existence of the twin connection. It was a simple and inexpensive experiment that could be repeated anywhere in a couple of hours, though it apparently never has been.

In 1976, two four-year-old twins, Silvia and Marta Landa, found their way into their local newspaper. The reason for their sudden fame was that Marta had burned her hand on a clothes iron. Normally this would hardly have been worth reporting, but what was newsworthy was the fact that as a large red blister was forming on her hand, an identical one was appearing on Silvia's – although she was on a visit to her grandparents in Logroño at the time. She had also felt a sharp pain, and was taken to a doctor who put some ointment on the wound. When the two little girls were reunited, their parents noted that their blisters were the same size, and on the same part of the same hand.

The Landas were getting used to this kind of thing, being already convinced that their daughters were exceptionally coincidence-prone. They first time they noticed this was when a doctor called to see Marta, who had tonsillitis and was running a temperature of 102. Silvia did not look very well either, so the doctor took her temperature and found it was also 102. This would have been quite normal if there as anything wrong with her tonsils, but as the doctor found, there wasn't.

The girls' mother would always give both of them the same medicine even if only one of them seemed to need it – she could be sure that the other would develop the same symptoms eventually, which, as I have said, would be quite normal assuming the disease had an internal cause. She had also noticed something harder to explain: if one of them had an accident the other seemed aware of it wherever she happened to be at the time. On one occasion they came home in their car, and Marta hopped out and ran into the house, but suddenly complained that she couldn't move her foot. It turned out that Silvia had got into a tangle with the seat belt and her foot was stuck in it. Then there was the time one of them had done something naughty and was given a smack, whereupon the other one, who was out of sight, promptly burst into tears.

The newspaper cutting found its way to the Madrid office of the Spanish Parapsychology Society, and a group of its members decided this was a case worth following up. It seemed to be generally accepted in Spain that there was a special twin connection, but nobody had ever bothered to investigate it properly any more than they had anywhere else. So they assembled a team of no fewer than nine psychologists, psychiatrists and doctors and descended on the Landas' house. It was probably the first time that researchers anywhere had gone into the field to study telepathy in its natural habitat, and their initiative was well rewarded.[1]

They had hardly arrived when they were given a demonstration of the kind of thing that kept happening to the little twins, when Marta banged her head on something and Silvia, but apparently not Marta, began to cry. (Another unwitting participant in my bang-on-the-head experiment!) The researchers then got to work on an ingenious series of tests that were disguised as either games or a routine medical check-up of the kind to which the girls must have been accustomed. Thus they had no idea that they were taking part in a psi experiment.

Marta seemed to be the dominant member of the pair, so they decided to make her the sender. Silvia, acting as receiver, went up to the second floor with her father and some of the researchers while Marta stayed on the ground floor with her mother and the rest of the team. Everything that happened on both floors was filmed and tape-recorded.

For the first test, psychologist Jordán Pena decided to have a bit of fun with a glove puppet, which gave him the chance to show Marta his skill as a ventriloquist. Silvia was given an identical puppet but was not given a similar demonstration. At one point, Marta grabbed the puppet and threw it at the investigator, whereupon Silvia did likewise with hers.

Next, one of the team's doctors began the check-up tests by shining a bright light into Marta's left eye. When she had done this four times, Silvia began to blink rapidly as if trying to avoid a bright light. Then the doctor gave Marta the knee-jerk reflex test, tapping her left leg three times. This turned out to be the most successful of the tests, because Silvia began to twitch her left leg so insistently that her father, who had no idea what was going on downstairs, had to hold it still.

Next, Marta was given some 'highly concentrated perfume' to smell and as she did so, Silvia shook her head and put a hand over her nose. Finally, there were a couple more game tests in which the girls, still in different rooms, were asked to arrange seven coloured discs in any order they liked, which they both did in exactly the same order. Then they were asked to do the same with a set of pictures numbered from one to six.

This produced an interesting result, Marta's sequence of choices being 4, 3, 1, 2, 5, 6 and Silvia's 3, 4, 2, 1, 5, 6, her first and second pairs being the reverse of her sister's. This suggests that the girls might have been 'mirror twins' – some twins divide later than others and it seems that if egg division takes place in the second week rather than the first, the twins will tend to be differently handed or have their hair parting on opposite sides. Whether this late division makes them more telepathy-prone or less remains to be studied.

The Madrid team rated the results of the knee-jerk test as

'highly positive', and all the others 'positive' except the last one which was merely 'relatively significant'. Finally, they gave each of the girls a Rorschach or ink-blot test, which revealed that they were definitely extraverts by nature, as were the high-scoring twins tested by Charlesworth and Robichon. A picture of the ideal telepathy pair is beginning to emerge.

As always, the Spanish report had its imperfections. It was very short, the actual experiments being described with minimal brevity – one of them in only three words – yet if any research ever cried out to be repeated, this is it. It confirms the well-established finding that young children are more telepathy-prone than adults, probably because they have no resistance to it and simply take it as natural, losing the ability once their sceptical parents or teachers have explained that it is impossible.

Psychologist Ernesto Spinelli of the University of Surrey tested a large number of people aged from three to 70 for telepathy, and found that those over eight scored close to chance while those under eight scored 'highly significantly above chance'.[2] There was a strong peak at age three, after which psi ability declined steadily until it reached chance level around age eight. He also found something surprising: an inverse correlation between children's intellectual development and their telepathic faculty. So it now seems the ideal subjects for telepathy tests are extravert identical twins aged under eight who are somewhat stupid.

TELEPATHY SAVES A LIFE

The Landa twins are not the youngest on record to have shown an ability to communicate at a distance. I have a case in my own file in which this was done by a pair of twins aged just three days. Their mother, Anna Powles, told me what happened:

I found it easier to feed them during the night in my bed. I would prop myself up with pillows, and this particular time I had one twin in front of me. My other son who, I might add, weighed only five pounds, lay on a pillow to the left of me.

As I proceeded to take the nappy off Ricky and to clean him, he suddenly started to scream. Now, even though he was only three days old he was a really good baby, as was his brother. I thought, 'Now what's the matter with you? There's nothing wrong – you have been fed and winded.' Suddenly he started to shake his whole body. I knew he wasn't having a fit, and suddenly I thought 'Twins relay messages to each other.'

Some mothers, no doubt, would never have had such a thought, and it is just as well that Mrs Powles did have it:

I looked down to Damien and to my horror he wasn't there. I twisted round and there he was face down in the pillows behind me. I grabbed hold of his baby-gro and he was blue in the face and his mouth clamped shut

The baby was in the process of suffocating to death, and only prompt and efficient action by both his mother and her older daughter saved the day, one administering artificial respiration and the other calling an ambulance. Mrs Powles concludes:

Without a doubt, Ricky saved his brother's life. Had it not been for him screaming and shaking, I never would have looked for Damien until I had finished with Ricky, and by then it would have been too late.

SYNCHRONIZED SLEEP

Perhaps telepathy should be taken rather more seriously than it is by some, if it can save lives? I was not surprised to learn that Mrs Powles had plenty of previous experience of it. She would always know, she assured me, when her former husband was about to come home, although he did not have a regular time. (Several friends of mine have told me the same thing.) She later gave me a rather delightful account of a more peaceful incident than the one above:

One evening my boys fell asleep on the sofa with me. They were either end, and I sat in the middle. Neither was touching the other. I sat for ten minutes until I became spooked watching them in their sleep. One would move a finger, I would turn to look at the other and he would move the same finger. This went on, as I say, for ten minutes – feet, hands, thumbs, no matter which one moved the other did the identical. I often look in on them when they are asleep, and when one rouses you can be sure the other does. I wonder, are they dreaming the same dream or do they just pick up on each other's movements even though they are asleep?

At least one pair of twins do have the same dreams. A mother of seven-year-old girls told me that the previous day she had been in the bathroom with one of them who had described a very peculiar dream she had just had, which went something like this:

I got on the bus and all the people in it were dead, and I tried to buy a ticket but the driver said I can't because he hasn't got any money. Then we got off and the boys chased us in the park.

A few minutes later the other girl, who had not been in the bathroom, described exactly the same dream. A couple of days later I was able to meet the twins and I asked them if they could remember their funny bus dream. They could indeed, and told me the same as their mother had told me, one after the other, in practically the same words. I asked them if they could remember any other funny dreams, and they told me about a rather scary one in which a big owl had got into their room and was staring at them.

'Do you always have the same dreams?' I asked them.

'Yes!' they replied without hesitation, in unison.

How much evidence of this kind goes unrecorded, one wonders, simply because nobody looks for it? French sleep researcher Michel Jouvet has done a good deal of work with sleeping twins, monitoring their brainwaves all night and reporting that 'we found essentially the same organization of sleep – the same timing, the same duration of REM [rapid eye movement, indicating the dream state], and so on.'[3] Jouvet never got around to asking his twin subjects if they had the same dreams, though he mentioned the fact that one or two of them had spontaneously told him that they had. It should be quite easy to get two twins to sleep in separate rooms, wake them up after an REM period and ask them to describe the dream they have just had as is done in conventional dream studies. Yet, as I was to find again and again, non-parapsychologists just do not do this kind of thing. It is taboo.

The nearest any of them seems to have got to it was at Minnesota, where a rather half-hearted attempt was made to study dream communication between twins as part of a general survey of twin brainwave similarities. These revealed 'striking within-pair similarity' in the EEG (brainwave) spectra of the identicals, especially in the alpha wave band of about 7 to 13 cycles per second, which is associated with psi-conducive states of mind. Those of the non-identicals, on the other hand, were no more similar than those of non-twin couples.

This discovery led the researchers to speculate that some kind of resonance effect was at work, and if brainwaves look as though they are resonating with each other the logical next step would be to see if information could be transferred. Psychologist David Lykken monitored a pair of identicals sleeping in separate rooms, and every now and then he played a tape-recording of each twin calling out the name of her sister. The idea was to see if the sleeping twin whose name was being called would respond in any way, and at first it seemed that she did, though we are not told how.

However, Lykken claimed to have found that this was due to some unspecified malfunction in his computer, and apparently decided not to try again. This was possibly the first and last time anybody at Minnesota came anywhere near studying telepathy, and Lykken does not even mention the aborted experiment in his 1982 paper on his brainwave resonance work. It was only made known 15 years later by author Lawrence Wright, to whom he mentioned it in an interview.[4]

STRONG AND WEAK SIGNALS

The word resonance has many meanings, one of which conveys the idea that something can happen as a result of something else being done at a distance, as when a piano string locks on to a signal from a tuning fork. How this can explain telepathy is far from clear (though I hope it will become slightly clearer by the end of this book), but for the time being we can say that just as if something looks like a duck and goes quack quack it probably is a duck, so an effect that looks like resonance might be just that.

If it is, or something like it, we can expect information to be exchanged, which in the case of identical twins it definitely is, especially when they are children. A mother of five-month-old boys has told me what happened when she took them to be inoculated:

A friend was holding Connor comfortably on her lap and I had Jack. Just as the paediatrician stuck the needle in Jack, Connor cried out. Jack subsequently cried a little. It may have been coincidence, but Connor had no reason to complain as he was comfortable.

Connor might have been able to see Jack, of course, and been frightened when somebody stuck a needle into him, though I doubt if a five-month-old knows what a needle is. We could dismiss a case like this as a 'one-off' due to that old favourite, coincidence, but for the fact that it is not a one-off. Here is another such case again involving twins less than a year old, in which one was well out of sight of the other. One of them, Paul, had been admitted to Warrington Hospital, where he had to be given intravenous injections of antibiotics every four hours. His mother recalls:

Paul had a needle in his hand through which the antibiotic was pumped slowly over about 30 minutes so as not to cause too much pain. Although this was uncomfortable, it did not seem to bother him too much.

I stayed in the hospital with Paul while my husband stayed at home with Phillip. On the first night, his injection was due at 6 p.m. and again at 10 p.m. The 6 p.m. one went fine, but a different nurse came to do the 10 p.m. one – instead of giving it to him via the machine she injected it into the needle on the back of his hand, and he screamed in a way I had never heard before or since. His pain lasted about 15 minutes before he calmed down.

Next morning when my husband arrived I asked him whether [our other] children had been all right without me and whether Phillip had been OK without Paul. He said they had except that at 10 o'clock, just as the news came on, Phillip had suddenly woken up and had screamed inconsolably for about a quarter of an hour. My husband had been unable to quiet him. Then he stopped as suddenly as he had started, and went back to sleep. We often wonder whether Phillip felt Paul's pain in some way.

To judge from this very precise account, it certainly sounds like it, but we cannot ask a baby aged five months for his version of events. Luckily, we have numerous cases in which older children were able to describe the signals of pain or danger they picked up. Here is one from a radio phone-in programme in which sceptical author Peter Watson was taking part.[5] A caller named Ted had this to say about his twin boys:

> *When they were young – there was one instance one Saturday lunchtime – one was in the kitchen having his lunch, the other one was playing outside. Now there's no way we can see from our kitchen to the front gate, yet we heard this scream and Nicholas, who was sitting in the kitchen, said, 'Quick, Michael's trapped his knee in the gate,' and sure enough he had slipped and his knee was trapped in the paling of the gate.*

'How often did they trap their knees in that gate?' the presenter asked. Obviously if Michael did this regularly, Nicholas could reasonably have guessed that he had done it again when he heard him scream.

'They never have done, before or since,' Ted replied.

'So you believe that there is something definitely spooky between them?'

'Well, I don't know. There certainly is an affinity which is – well, I can't understand it.'

Peter Watson, however, was unimpressed by this particular scintilla of evidence for anomalous communication between twins. 'It may have been a guess,' he said. 'One must always be sceptical in these cases – that he knew roughly where his twin was playing and he knew roughly what kind of injury he might have sustained.'

One must indeed be sceptical in the face of evidence of any kind, but one should remember that the word comes from the Greek verb *skeptesthai*, which means 'to examine'. True scepticism is about careful examination and not rejection out of hand. However, when the evidence begins to pile up, with similar incidents being reported from people who could never have had any contact with each other, it becomes more likely that it is true.

An American, Mrs Laura Helser, seems to have made another lucky guess:

When we were quite small, I was in the kitchen with Mother one day, and suddenly I said 'Hurry, Elizabeth has fallen off Jack's bicycle and hurt her knee!' Without doubting, Mother followed, and I ran down the street because I knew just where she was. We found her still lying on the ground where she had fallen.[6]

Here is another case taken verbatim from a radio interview between BBC science correspondent James Wilkinson and twins Lorna and Madeleine Greensmith from Welwyn, Hertfordshire.[vii] It is a valuable one, since we have evidence from both sender and receiver.

MG: When we were about eight years old, I was playing in the playground with a friend and I was pushed into the wall, and I cracked half my tooth off. Meanwhile, Lorna was having lunch in the refectory, and she suddenly got very anxious and felt something was wrong with me. I was in quite a lot of pain, bleeding and everything, and I was taken to the first-aid room, and Lorna – much against all the efforts of our friends to try and calm her down – felt she just had to come and find where I was and find if I was OK.

LG [asked how she had felt at the time]: Panic-stricken. There was no particular reason for me to suddenly feel that way because I was just eating my dinner.

JW: You went in search of your sister?

LG: Yes, I immediately went to try and find her. The fact that I couldn't find her for a while just made my feeling worse that

*there was something wrong, and when I did find her in the
end, there was something wrong.*

Indeed there was, and it is interesting that Lorna did not report
feeling any pain, as other twins have done on similar occasions,
also that her telepathic skill does not seem to have been much help
when she was looking for her sister. The signal seems to be picked
up in all kinds of ways, sometimes very clearly as in Mrs Helser's
case mentioned above, sometimes not so clearly, as with Lorna and
Madeleine, and sometimes in a very unclear and indirect way, as in
another case from a radio interview in which a woman recalled
what she felt one evening:

*I had a feeling that I must ring [my sister], and actually I was
working in London and had to walk to a phone box quite a
long way to ring her, about a mile in the dark, in a sort of
unknown bit of London, and when I got into the phone box
I suddenly felt I just couldn't – I wasn't strong enough myself
to cope with her unhappiness at that particular moment, and
I walked away without phoning, and that was the night she
died.*[8]

In this case from my own collection, the telepathic signal was
weaker still:

*In the summer of 1997 my sister Lucy went to live in Japan.
In January of this year [1999] I fell pregnant, but before I
knew about it Lucy phoned with a rather strange request. She
told me that for no reason at all her breasts had become tender
and slightly swollen, and could I buy her some bras and send
them out to her? Apparently Japanese bras aren't suitable for
Westerners! She has since told me that later on that day she
suddenly thought 'What if Joanna's pregnant?' By our next
conversation, within the next day or two, I was able to*

*confirm that I was, and that was that. That's all there is to it
– strange but true.*

Sometimes there is no signal at all when we might expect there to
be one. Helen and Margaret Campbell were very similar identical
twins, though they went their own ways and did their best to assert
their independence.[ix] Even so, Helen recalls that 'Margaret and I
were close in our minds at times. Although we were hundreds of
miles apart we would often buy exactly the same shoes and other
articles.' Yet when Margaret's body was found on a beach,
apparently having been there for some time, Helen does not report
receiving any impressions at all, even though her sister had clearly
been in a disturbed mental state and may have committed suicide.
(The case was never solved.)

MAKING WAVES

When the signal is strong, however, is clear that, as Mary
Rosambeau put it after receiving nearly 200 reports of telepathy
from twins:

*Pain, distress and disaster seem to make the waves that the
sensitive pick up. No one reports a sudden access of joy which
is later found to have coincided with their twin having won a
million pounds.*[10]

A detailed example of such wave-reception at full strength was
given to me in April 2002 by Aily Biggs, a London banker, and her
twin sister Dr Alison Armour, a hospital doctor in Scotland. Aily
told me how when a teenager she had been out in the hills above
her home town of Greenock collecting soil samples for a school
project. It was early evening and very misty as she headed down the
narrow and deserted country road towards the spot where her
father was to pick her up.

I was walking down the road and a car came up, a yellow Viva, and it passed me. I didn't think anything of it, but then it came back – and then it came back up again, which I thought was very strange.

I was in a really uptight state, highly adrenalized. I'd never experienced anything like it. I just thought, 'I've got to run.' As I was running, which I remember very vividly, thinking the car was coming back to get me, and thinking 'Alison, if there's anything you can do, tell Dad to come quick!'

Alison was at home, in the room she shared with her sister. She was studying for an important exam, buried in a book, when, as she told me:

All of a sudden the atmosphere in the whole room changed. It was as if Aily was in the room – I wasn't on my own any more. The door was closed, but I remember feeling something beside me, it was almost as if Aily was standing there. It was quite a scary feeling [which she had not had before or since]. I didn't look up, but I got the impression there was a form like Aily standing beside me. It was accompanied by a feeling of real panic – like 'Get Dad! Get Dad!' I suddenly knew there was something wrong with Aily.

Alison cannot recall today exactly what she did, but Aily can. According to her, the first thing her twin said when they were reunited was 'All I got was a yellow car door, and "Tell Dad to come quickly."' Which he did.

Alison can, however, recall other instances on which both she and her sister picked up each other's pains. Once, she was out running when she tripped in a pothole and fell, spraining her ankle. At the same time, Aily felt a sudden burning sensation starting in her feet and spreading all over her. On another occasion it was Alison's turn to feel sudden pain for no obvious reason, in this case in her nose. She had hoped to have an early night, and was in bed at about half-past nine when the pain became so severe that she had to get up and take a painkiller.

Meanwhile, some 60 miles away, Aily was swimming in a pool in Edinburgh when another swimmer suddenly shot up from the bottom of the pool and rammed her in the face, breaking her nose. Yes, she said, it would have been about 9.30.

TIP OF THE ICEBERG

The twin connection, by means of which one mind seems to be expressing itself in two bodies, involves more than shared experience of pain or strong emotions, as in the above examples. It also includes similarity of likes, dislikes, behaviour and actions such as writing identical exam papers, buying the same dress or present, or choosing the same name for a child or a pet. Some of these can easily be put down to genetic causes – after all, two people who are virtually identical are likely to have the same tastes and abilities; some may be no more than coincidence, which I discuss in the following chapter, but there remains a solid core of evidence for a connection that cannot be explained in terms of presently accepted science.

Not all my twin informants have been as articulate and cooperative as the two just mentioned. Here is an example of one of my failed investigations, of which there were quite a few. A friend had mentioned meeting a twin in her village who had experience of what sounded like telepathy, so I asked her if she could get more out of him. It might not be easy, I warned her. She replied:

He affirmed the fact that there have been more than a few times when he and his identical twin have had instant knowledge of the other's illness or discomfort, etc. But, as you said, he is very reticent and mysterious about the whole matter, and so I gave it up as a bad job.

The evidence presented in this book, then, may be no more than the proverbial tip of a huge iceberg. Much of it would never have come to light if I had not asked for it, and there might have been more of it if some twins did not have a curiously ambivalent attitude to the subject of telepathy. I have even heard one twin giving an account of what sounded like a clear case of feeling her sister's pain at a distance, but rejecting the idea of telepathy, ESP, psi or whatever out of hand. Asked what else could explain her experience, she replied, as if she had been asked a really daft question:

'It's because we're twins.'

CHAPTER 5

A SORT OF CAMOUFLAGE

The Casablanca Effect

Of all the gin joints in all the towns in all the world, she walks into mine.

Coincidences do indeed happen, though they are not always as dramatic as Ingrid Bergman's reunion with Humphrey Bogart in *Casablanca*. One of the first things the Minnesota team noticed when they began to study separated and reunited twins was that the identicals seemed much more coincidence-prone than the non-identicals. Even when separated at birth and being unaware that they were twins until late in life, some pairs were found to have led almost identical lives in many respects. They had married similar men, had the same number of children of the same sex, often giving them the same names, and had the same tastes and preferences in everything from food and clothing to books and hobbies.

Some had their own idiosyncrasies: each of one pair could bathe in the sea only if she walked in backwards. Each of another pair insisted on having the door left open when they were being questioned. Yet the champions of coincidence must be the British sisters Barbara Herbert and Daphne Goodship, known at Minnesota as the Giggle Sisters for their high spirits and infectious laughter. They met for the first time when they were 40, following a heroic legal battle by Barbara to be reunited with her long-lost twin.

When they compared notes, they found they shared at least 30 close similarities, not only in their tastes for food, drink, books and

68

clothes, but also in events in their lives. Both, for instance, had met their future husbands at a dance in their local Town Hall when they were 16. Both had also fallen down stairs in the same year, damaging their ankles. Since then, neither can walk down a flight of stairs without clutching the banister.

One of their most spectacular coincidences took place at Minnesota when each was asked, separately, to write any sentence they liked so that their handwriting could be compared. Like many, perhaps, they chose to write 'The cat sat on the mat.' At least, that is what they meant to write, but both misspelled the second word as 'cas'. They were constantly being told by the interviewers after replying to a question that 'your sister just said that'.

As Barbara Herbert told me in 2000, the coincidences are still going on. When their granddaughters were born, both sisters knitted cardigans of the same colour and pattern. Both wrote to the same women's magazine on the same day to ask the same question, neither telling the other that she had done so. When Barbara went to a London station to meet her twin for the first time, she stood on the platform and when the train came to a halt, Daphne stepped out of the door right in front of her. They were not wearing the same clothes, she told me, but Daphne arrived at the big family reunion party a few weeks later wearing a beige dress and a brown jacket – exactly what Barbara was wearing.

In their regular telephone chats they frequently learn that they have both just cooked identical meals or just had a sardine sandwich and glass of cider. They both won £10 on the National Lottery in the same week. When Daphne won a bottle of Avon perfume in a raffle, Barbara won a prize in a draw run by her local Avon lady.

Yet in spite of this persistent coincidence-proneness – they even both have mothers-in-law named Maud who were born on the same day of the same year – this is one pair of identicals who do not have any experience of telepathy although this, Barbara assured me, was the only thing they had never been tested for, at Minnesota or anywhere else.

They have, however, been tested for intelligence, initially at Minnesota and several years later in England. On each occasion their IQ scores were just one point apart, which is interesting in view of the fact that they were brought up in very different circumstances, the parents who adopted one twin being much better off than those who adopted the other. Nature, in their case at least, seems to have been more important than nurture.

THINKING THE UNTHINKABLE

Coincidence has been the subject of several books, notably those by C. G. Jung, Arthur Koestler and Brian Inglis,[1] but after reading them I find I can only comment, 'Goodness, how strange' and agree with Inglis that 'coincidences are not an attractive subject for scientific research' for the simple reason that they can be impossible to prove or disprove, although Jung did his best to make a case for what he called synchronicities, or meaningful coincidences resulting from an 'acausal connecting principle'. He made a point that is very relevant to twin studies:

Meaningful coincidences are thinkable as pure chance. But the more they multiply and the greater and more exact the correspondence is, the more their probability sinks and their unthinkability increases until they can no longer be regarded as pure chance, but, for lack of a causal explanation, have to be thought of as meaningful arrangements.[2]

Jung was himself involved in one of his most often quoted coincidences. This took place in 1909 when he went to visit his mentor, Sigmund Freud, and was having an argument about psychic phenomena, for which Freud had little time. The argument became quite heated and Jung had a job to control himself. Indeed, he began to get heated as well, feeling as if his diaphragm was becoming red hot, like 'a glowing vault'. Both men were then startled by a loud bang coming from a bookcase.

'There,' said Jung, 'that is an example of a so-called catalytic exteriorization phenomenon,' to which Freud replied, 'Oh come, that is sheer bosh.' No it wasn't, said Jung, and to prove it he predicted that there would be another big bang in a moment, as indeed there was.

'To this day,' he wrote many years later, 'I do not know what gave me this certainty. But I knew beyond all doubt the report would come again.'[3]

What is interesting about Jung's experience (and he had several similar ones in his own home, during one of which a heavy table split in two) was his certainty that something more than chance was at work. This is just what we find when a twin *knows* there is something wrong with the other one, as in this case which I received from a young American academic:

I will highlight one experience in which I knew my twin sister was in danger many miles away. While an undergraduate student at Stony Brook University I awoke from a deep sleep at 6 a.m. New York time. I cried out that my twin sister, who was 3,000 miles away, was in trouble and told my roommate what had happened. Concerned, I called my mother and found out that at 3 a.m. Arizona time a bomb placed in a car had exploded outside my sister's apartment, shattering her window. My sister and her husband rushed out of their apartment. There is a three-hour time difference between New York and Arizona so my awakening with the awareness that my twin sister was in trouble coincided with the explosion.

She told me that she had had other experiences of knowing when her sister was in trouble, and her sister had had similar experiences involving her. I find it impossible not to be convinced by this account of what cannot reasonably be dismissed as a coincidence.

The woman had nothing to gain by making it all up, and asked not to be named here, because apparently having telepathic experience with your sister puts your academic career at risk.

DOUBTS REMAIN

There are those, however, who are far from convinced by evidence of this quality. In a 1987 *Newsweek* cover story on twins, the reporters discovered that researchers had been given 'dozens' of accounts suggestive of telepathy over the years, most of them involving injury, birth or death.[4] They heard one such report directly from an engineer named Donald Keith, who described how he had been walking along a corridor in his Rockville, Maryland, office 'when he suddenly experienced a series of sharp pains like jolts of electricity in his groin'. Phoning his twin brother in Chicago later that day, he learned that he had just injured a groin muscle. 'The hair on the back of my neck stood straight up,' Mr Keith recalled.

The hairs of psychologists, however, remain undisturbed, as the *Newsweek* reporters found:

Nancy Segal, co-director of an ongoing eight-year study of twins at the University of Minnesota, says she doesn't 'doubt the reality of [telepathy]', since the stories are too numerous to be total fabrications. But she is reluctant to label them paranormal. She notes that researchers 'never hear of the cases where one twin is sure the other is lying dead in the gutter, and he isn't'. And since twins think about each other more than other siblings, experiences labelled ESP may be just coincidences.

Dr Segal is almost certainly right in claiming that we never hear of cases like the one she describes. This could be for a very simple reason – there are no such cases and never have been.

There are, however, plenty of cases like that of Marcus and Alex

Lewis.[5] Marcus once telephoned his mother at 2 a.m. apparently for no other reason than to ask if his twin Alex was all right. His mother sleepily assured him that he was as far as she knew and went back to sleep. Twenty minutes later she was woken up again, this time by a hospital, to which Alex had just been taken following a serious motorcycle accident. He may well have been lying in a gutter, though luckily not dead, when Marcus rang his mother to ask about him. How many more cases of this kind do there have to be before the research community takes notice?

At the risk of overloading readers with yet more evidence, and of upsetting those who – like the late Sam Goldwyn – have made up their minds and don't want to be confused with facts, here is a brief selection of some cases from the last half of the 20th century for which chance coincidence seems an unlikely explanation. As might be expected, they all involve pain, violence or sudden death.[6]

* Alice Lambe, aged 20, of Springfield, Illinois, was reading at home one afternoon in 1948 when she felt a massive blow on her left side which made her fall off her chair and pass out. Her father heard her cry out, 'Something's happened to Dianne,' just before she lost consciousness. So it had – her twin was in a train crash 70 miles away that left her with two fractured ribs, on her left side.

  There was more. Alice's pain would not go away and she was unable to go to work for three weeks, the same period that Dianne spent in hospital. The pain became so severe that she was x-rayed and found to have two fractured ribs – the same ones as her sister and in the same places.

* In 1975, a hospital worker named Nita Hust felt sudden pains in her left leg, and found that bruises had appeared on the left side of her body. The matron saw some of them appear spontaneously. At about the same time, Nita's twin Nettie Porter was involved in a car crash 400 miles away in which she bruised herself in exactly the same places.

* The saddest case of this kind was described by an Australian woman named Joyce Crominski. I would find her story hard to believe were it not for the fact that she wrote an account of it herself and sent it to an Australian magazine. It was not the kind of story you would expect somebody to invent about their own family. It concerned her twin sisters Helen and Peg who apparently died within minutes of each other in very unusual circumstances. Again, a car crash was involved, with Peg dying in the ambulance that was taking her to hospital, her chest crushed by the steering wheel, and Helen waking up with a loud scream and complaining of a severe pain in her chest. She too was rushed to hospital, but like her twin she died before she got there.

* By way of contrast, here is a case from 1980 that seems to provide evidence against telepathy. George and Stephen Youngblood set off one day on their motorcycles, heading in opposite directions, and after zooming round some side roads in Missouri they were abruptly brought together in a head-on collision in which Stephen was killed. If we wonder why neither seems to have been aware of the approach of the other, we should remember that receivers of a telepathic message are almost invariably in a relaxed state and not tearing around on motorbikes or anything like that.

* Finally, a case described to me in 1999 by a senior consultant obstetrician, which I mentioned briefly in Chapter 1. He told me he had been attending to a patient in England who was having a difficult and painful period of labour, and he had decided to perform a Caesarian section. He was just about to do this when his patient's sister telephoned from Australia begging him to operate as soon as he could 'because I can't stand the pain'. She was aware that her sister was pregnant, I gathered, but had not been told that she needed an emergency operation. Later, the consultant received a letter from Australia thanking him and saying she felt fine again. He seemed to think this kind of thing was quite normal with twins.

Yet can we be sure that all cases of this kind show telepathy in action? It seems quite common for similar pain-sharing, especially labour pain, to be reported by non-identicals, non-twins and even husbands. I have been given a vivid account of this by a man I know well. He was aware, of course, when his wife was expecting, but we have at least one well-documented case in which a twin felt pain when she had no idea that her sister, on the other side of the Atlantic, was in the process of giving birth. The twins concerned were Gloria Vanderbilt and Thelma Furness, whose simultaneous gift-buying I mentioned earlier.

When Lady Furness was expecting her baby, she was in Europe and Gloria was in New York. The baby was due in May and Gloria was planning to come over to be with her sister when it arrived. However, in late March she was about to go out to lunch when:

> *I developed abdominal pains, so severe in fact that I had my maid telephone to say I should have to cancel. I remember saying to her… that if I didn't know such a thing was out of the question, I would think I was having a baby.*

She took a sedative and managed to get a few hours' sleep, feeling perfectly normal again when she woke up. She soon discovered why. On the bedside table was a cable from Lord Furness announcing the premature birth of Thelma's son.[7]

Self-suggestion was clearly not at work in this case, so why should we assume that it ever is? Why should we assume that cases of identical gift-buying or exam-writing are merely due to 'genetic underpinning' or some such non-explanatory jargon? It may seem normal for twins to buy each other identical presents, since they are bound to know that their twins will probably like something they like themselves, yet there must be any number of things twins would like to give or be given. It does seem 'unthinkable' that of all the gifts in all the gift shops in town, again and again twins choose the same ones.

They did it once more in December 2001. On Christmas Eve I took part in a programme on Talksport Radio hosted by Uri Geller in which I mentioned my twin research and guessed that some twins would probably be giving and receiving identical presents for Christmas. I might have added that since the festival of Hanukkah had ended the previous week, some Jewish twins might just have done so.

They had. On his way home after the show, Uri received a call from a friend in Belgium, to whom he happened to mention my prediction. 'Oh yes,' said the man, 'I've got twin sons and they just did that!' It seems that one, in Tel Aviv, had been to two shops to buy a present for his brother without finding anything he liked, and had finally gone to a third shop and chosen a wallet from a selection of seven or eight different colours.

At exactly the same time, or very near to it, the twin 1,800 miles away in Antwerp had bought an identical wallet – same make, same colour. Clearly, the Casablanca Effect is universal.

JUST ANOTHER COINCIDENCE?

Peter Watson, to his credit, looked at some length into the subject of coincidence in general and between twins in particular. He worked out the mathematical probability of some of the similarities reported by the Minnesota team, finding that in many cases this was close to the probability, for example, of being killed in a road accident. However he concedes that twins experience coincidence (assuming that is all it is) in more ways than non-twins do, and he asks a good question: 'Just how rare does something have to be for it to defy the laws of nature?'[8]

He admits that there is no ready answer. Very improbable events do occur. (At least three have happened to me; they were too complicated to include here but two of them have been published in full.) Our chance of winning the National Lottery has been estimated at about one in 14 million, yet somebody usually does win it and the odds are just the same for the winners as for everybody else. As far as I know, nobody has yet won it five or ten times, yet in effect this is what many twins have done by having far more than their fair share of synchronous events.

Although Watson has no time for telepathy and clearly supports the 'all in the genes' school, he has to admit that, 'It still seems that the odds against whole chains of coincidences are so huge that something about human behaviour is being reflected in the Minnesota findings.' It is indeed, even more strikingly so in the everyday lives of twins outside the laboratory.

What is reflected in my findings is very clear: some twin coincidences are indeed due to genetic underpinning and some are not, and it is usually easy to tell which is which. For example, when 17-year-old Jonathan Floyd felt sudden pains in his stomach and had to have his appendix removed, it was not surprising that his brother Jason, 300 miles away, also had to have an emergency appendectomy less than a day later. They had, as one of them put it, been 'medical blueprints of each other' all their lives, which is what one would expect if they are genetically identical.[9]

Yet they had also been 'accident blueprints'. When he was four, Jason fell through a window and had to have a head wound stitched up. Three days later Jonathan fell through the same window and had to have the same number of stitches in the same place. Is there a gene for falling through windows, I wonder?

Was there a genetic cause for six-year-old Liam and Aaron Lynch to be admitted to Wycombe General Hospital with broken collar bones within half an hour of each other?[10] Liam had been climbing a fence, but Aaron had tripped and fallen down as he was running. How can genetics explain why John and Michael Atkins both fell and broke legs at exactly the same time while skiing on different glaciers in the Alps, well out of sight of each other?[11]

'When we compared notes,' John told a reporter, 'we discovered we had both slipped on the ice at exactly 12 midday.' He added, 'We are identical twins and often do the same things, but this is ridiculous!' Could it be that one of them fell first and actually caused the other to fall seconds later? We have plenty of cases in which pain was felt at a distance followed by bruises, blisters and broken bones, so if one of the Atkins brothers suddenly felt a sharp pain in the leg it would not be surprising if he then fell and really did break it.

Likewise, it is difficult to find a genetic explanation for the tragic case reported in March 2002 in which a pair of Finnish twins suffered fatal accidents within a couple of hours of each other.[12] It also stretches the 'just a coincidence' theory to unreasonable limits, involving as it did a triple coincidence in which both twins died on the same day, in the same circumstances, and in almost the same place. As described by police constable Mika Lindqvist:

The first brother died when he was crossing the road on his bike, and he didn't notice a truck that was coming. Two hours later, 1.5 kilometres south of where the first brother died, the second brother crossed the same road on his bike after a car had passed, but he didn't see the truck that came after the car, and was hit and died right away.

Even in cases in which genetics are clearly involved, there can also be suggestions of another factor at work. A particularly thoroughly investigated and documented case was that of Bobbie Jean and Betty Jo Eiler of Purlea, North Carolina, who died aged 31 at exactly (or very nearly) the same time in separate wards of the mental hospital where they had been undergoing treatment for schizophrenia.[13] A night nurse found Bobbie dead in her bed, lying on her side with her legs drawn up. Moments later, Betty was found lying on the floor in exactly the same position, also dead.

The coroner carried out thorough autopsies on both bodies, and declared that 'I found no demonstrable evidence of injury or disease that could cause death.' The twins' vital organs were then examined both by state forensic experts and by those of the Federal

Bureau of Investigation without any such evidence coming to light. The cause-of-death line on both death certificates was left blank.

People do not drop dead for no reason at all, and if one of the world's leading forensic laboratories could not find a normal cause, it seems reasonable to speculate that there may have been a paranormal one.

Synchronized Murder

Now for the strangest twin-coincidence case I have yet come across. Some readers may find it as hard to believe, as I did when I first read a short summary of it. (Later I obtained a copy of the original and detailed account.) Yet it provides compelling evidence that the first event involved was the direct cause of the second. The event concerned in this case, which took place in Romania in 1993, was murder.

The appropriately named Romulus and Remus Cozma were born in 1962.[14] According to their mother they were absolutely identical and very close to each other, displaying all the usual genetically driven concordances such as aches, pains and diseases. Yet they each could also feel the other's pain at a distance, such as when one or the other hurt himself playing football, as seems to have happened quite often. This went on when the boys were grown up and living in towns 500 miles apart, Romulus in Constanţa and Remus in Cluj. One day, Romulus fell and broke his right leg in a climbing accident, whereupon Remus promptly fell down stairs in his home and also broke his right leg.

In 1987 they both fell in love at about the same time with young women named Monica, though only Remus and his Monica got married. The marriage was not a success, and there were daily squabbles, neighbours recalling that it was Monica who did most of the yelling and screaming. She did more of this, for the last time, when Remus came home late one evening, evidently drunk. After what sounds like considerable provocation, he grabbed her round the neck and tried to strangle her. She managed to seize a kitchen knife and tried in turn to murder him, but he wrestled the knife from her and stuck it into her 12 times. Then he went to the local police station and confessed.

The following day, the police telephoned Remus's mother, who in turn called Romulus only to be told by his anxious landlady that, 'something must have happened to him' because 'two policemen came this very morning and took him away'.

The evening before, Romulus and his Monica had been to the cinema, then for a stroll in the park, and had sat down on a bench for what was to be their last embrace. Although they were not married they had always seemed to be a happy couple, and Romulus had absolutely no idea why he did what he did next, which was precisely what Remus had tried to do at, as far as is known, roughly the same time. He too grabbed his Monica around the throat, and unlike his brother he did indeed strangle her.

He seemed to have no motive at all. 'I don't know why I committed this monstrous crime. I felt impelled by an invisible force. I couldn't resist it,' he told police. 'Or,' he added enigmatically, 'perhaps I didn't want to?'

It emerged during the subsequent investigations that Remus's murder had probably been committed shortly before Romulus's, although understandably the exact times could not be known. It may sound improbable to suggest that Romulus picked up his brother's sudden fit of murderous rage and acted on it automatically without knowing why, yet in the absence of any known motive on his part this seems the most likely explanation. We can always duck the issue by complaining that we need more evidence, as could be said about all cases of any kind. We have, I suggest, quite enough evidence for the twin connection to draw some conclusions, which I leave until a later time when yet more evidence will have come in.

The Romanian case was one of those I am sure Jung would have rated as unthinkable, and it reminds me of Peter Watson's interesting, if somewhat inconclusive, summary of his study of coincidences:

Are all the coincidences that are being collected at Minnesota a sort of camouflage, a signal for something else that is going on at a deeper level?

I am sure he is right, and equally sure that what is going on is something innumerable people have experienced whether they are twins or, as I show in the following chapter, not. It is something that has been demonstrated again and again both in the laboratory and in real life and reported by reliable witnesses for at least 200 years. Something that continues to be demonstrated and reported regularly, with identical twins providing more than their fair share of such reports, despite the fact that there are still those who refuse to admit its existence, or even the possibility of its existence.

Something known, for want of a better word, as telepathy.

CHAPTER 6

TELEPATHY HAPPENS

ONE MIND, TWO BODIES

In 1784, the Marquis de Puységur, a French aristocrat, soldier and landowner, made an interesting discovery. He had studied the therapeutic practice of 'animal magnetism', or mesmerism as it was later known, with Franz Anton Mesmer himself, and was so impressed by his accidental discovery that he wrote a detailed account of it in a letter to one of his brothers. This was the first instance in modern times of well-documented and convincing evidence for what we now call telepathy.

The Marquis had been treating a young peasant on his estate at Buzancy, doing what Mesmer had taught him to do – passing his hands around the young man's body, without touching it but making 'passes' as he visualized a current of 'magnetic fluid' flowing through his hands into his patient. Suddenly, the man went spontaneously into what is believed to be the first reported hypnotic trance. It seemed he was not quite awake or quite asleep, but in a state somewhere in between. In the Marquis's words:

> *When he is magnetized, he is no longer a simple peasant who can barely answer a question; he is something I cannot describe. I have no need to speak to him, I think in front of him and he understands and answers me... When he wants to say more than I consider fit to be heard, I stop his ideas and sentences in the middle of a word, and I change his mind completely.*[1]

Puységur was more interested in treating his patients (free, incidentally) than in research of any kind, and although shelves of books were written about mesmerism, which gave way to hypnotism in the mid-19th century, it was to be nearly a hundred years until serious enquiry was made into 'thought transference', as I mentioned in Chapter 2. Other mesmerists, however, had made the same discovery as the Marquis, and one of the most articulate and scientifically minded was the Rev C. Hare Townshend, who included these perceptive comments on his own experiments in the transfer of taste and emotions in a book published in 1844:

> *We have seen that, in cases of mesmeric sympathy, the actual sensation of one person is transferred accurately to another; so also the mental action of the mesmeriser can – so to speak – perform motion in another... The inference is irresistible. One mind originates motion in two bodies... Whatever be the force which has moved the muscles of the one, precisely the same force is meted out to the muscles of the other.*[2]

However, just when it seemed that a new era of scientific investigation into the human mind and its hitherto hidden abilities was about to begin, two events that took place within a few years of each other served to postpone it for several decades. The first was the introduction in the mid-1840s of ether and chloroform as anaesthetics. Before then, having an operation could be a hideously painful affair, and one of the most dramatic discoveries the mesmerists made was that they could induce total anaesthesia – nobody is yet quite sure how. In 1829 Dr Jules Cloquet removed a breast tumour from a mesmerized woman who, he insisted, had shown no sign of feeling any pain at all. Cloquet duly reported this to the French Academy of Medicine, only to be told that his patient must have been just pretending not to suffer!

Other doctors performed similar pain-free operations, notably the Scotsman James Esdaile, who announced in 1847 that he had performed 300 major and several *thousand* minor operations using mesmerism. (Painless operations without anaesthesia are still being reported today, notably those by Spanish surgeon Dr Angel Escudero and the extraordinary Russian Anatoly Kashpirovsky.)[3] However, the new chemicals seemed an obvious improvement over mesmerism, which could take a long time to become effective, so mesmerism began to decline along with public interest in it.

The second event that radically polarized public opinion was the birth of spiritualism following the widely publicized outbreak in 1848 of what we would now call poltergeist phenomena in the Hydesville, NY, home of the Fox family. This created huge interest in what was assumed to be the spirit world, and before long tables were tilting all over Europe and the USA bringing messages from it. Not surprisingly there was a backlash from those who saw this as a return to the Dark Ages of superstition just when it seemed that a new age of scientific discovery was dawning. That psi research was already taboo in some circles was made clear by the novelist Catherine Crowe in her pioneering book *The Night-Side of Nature* (1848) in which she lambasted critics for their attitude towards new discoveries about the human mind:

The more important and the higher the results may be, the more angry they are with those who advocate them. They do not quarrel with a new metal or a new planet... and even a new comet or a new island stands a fair chance of being well received... while phrenology and mesmerism testify that any discovery tending to throw light on what most deeply concerns us, namely our own being, must be prepared to encounter a storm of angry persecution.[4]

Then as now! Another reason why many were put off the telepathic aspects of mesmerism was that by the 1840s, supposedly psychic phenomena were well established in the stage magician's repertoire. The handbill for a show in London in 1852 by Mademoiselle Prudence promised a demonstration of 'Mesmerism, Transmission of Thought, Illusions, Clairvoyance and Double Sight',[5] while the

French magician Jean Robert-Houdin had a stage routine in which his blindfolded son described objects given to his father by members of the audience, using not telepathy but cues from his father's verbal patter.[6]

It was hardly surprising, then, that telepathy came to be seen as synonymous with stage trickery, and that research into it, as I described in Chapter 2, was delayed for decades despite the efforts of Sir William Barrett. It did recover, however, chiefly because of the enthusiasm of the early SPR researchers, and it began to make progress in the 20th century once reliable and cheat-proof ways of testing for it had been developed by J. B. Rhine and his colleagues at Duke University.

Mental Radio

A new approach had been taken by a French engineer named René Warcollier, who decided to carry out experiments in the telepathic transmission of simple drawings.[7] He reported that many ordinary people could do this, but only if they were in the right frame of mind. The transmitter or sender had to concentrate hard but the receiver had to 'switch off', put the mind in neutral gear and just wait for the signal to come through. Warcollier was one of the first to show that tests could be done over long distances, between himself in France and colleagues in the USA.

His methods were adopted by the author of a book first published in 1930 (and still in print) called *Mental Radio*, which had a huge impact and remains one of the best how-to books on telepathy ever written. Some would have considered its author to be the last person who would have thought of writing about such a subject. He was the novelist and social crusader Upton Sinclair, best known for such radical novels as *The Jungle* and *Boston*.[8] And surely the last person who would have agreed to write an introduction to the book, which he reckoned 'deserves the most earnest consideration, not only of the laity but also of psychologists', was none other than Albert Einstein?

Sinclair's wife, Mary Craig Sinclair, had been experiencing telepathy since early childhood, and one day in 1928 the couple decided to put her skills to the test. Upton asked his brother-in-law Robert Irwin to do a drawing of anything he liked at his home in Pasadena, 40 miles from the Sinclairs' house in Long Beach, then to concentrate on it for 20 minutes or so. Meanwhile, Craig, as she was always called, would try to pick up what he was looking at.

She lay on a couch at the agreed time, closed her eyes and told her subconscious mind to bring her whatever was being sent out. Sure enough, something was brought. The same image kept floating in, and when she felt confident enough she picked up a pencil and wrote 'July 13, 1928. See a table fork. Nothing else.' What Irwin had drawn was unmistakably a table fork – and nothing else.

The Sinclairs eventually carried out a total of 290 tests in their home, with Upton doing the drawings and Craig, in another room, drawing or sometimes writing what she was picking up. The final score was:

Successes	65	(23%)
Partial successes	155	(53%)
Failures	70	(24%)

That is how Upton rated them, but in fact some of the partial successes were very intriguing, and tell us something about the way telepathy works. For instance, when Upton drew what he thought of as a volcano, with two sloping sides and a thick oval-shaped cloud of black smoke coming out of the top, Craig drew almost exactly the same picture, but sideways, deciding that it must be a beetle, the black oval shape being its body and the sides its antennae. She had fallen into the trap of what is now known as 'analytical overlay' whereby people pick up the right image but make the wrong assumptions as to what it is.

She was well aware of this by the time she wrote her own chapter in Upton's book, which contains instructions in how to receive telepathic messages that have yet to be surpassed for clarity and understanding of the process. The first thing, she wrote, was to relax into 'blankness', or what we now call the hypnagogic state – the state we are in just before we go to sleep, in which people often see images like little bits of dreams. She would then tell herself 'as if talking directly to another self' that she wanted to see what Upton was drawing next door.

Then relax into blankness again and hold blankness a few moments, then try gently, without straining, to see whatever forms may appear on the void into which you look with closed eyes. Do not try to conjure up something to see; just wait expectantly and let something come.

That really is all there is to it, and I know from my own experience that it works when you get the mental part right. I like to think of myself sitting in a huge open-air cinema on top of a hill staring at a big blue screen and waiting for the film to start without knowing or particularly caring what it will be.

Upton Sinclair was in no doubt as to what his wife had taught him: 'I tell you,' he wrote, 'and because it is so important, I put it in capital letters: TELEPATHY HAPPENS.' Even so, he was objective enough to admit that 'I don't like to believe in telepathy because I don't know what to make of it, and I don't know to what view of the universe it will lead me.' Craig, on the other hand, had no doubts as to what kind of view she was led to. If telepathy was real, she wrote, then 'my mind is not my own… I and the universe of men are one.'

Sinclair, despite his high profile as a socialist, did not escape the ridicule that anybody getting involved with telepathy (or any other kind of psi phenomenon) has to accept as coming with the job. A Boston newspaper headline greeted his book with the headline 'Sinclair Goes Spooky', and one of his left-wing friends told him after reading the manuscript that he could not accept the existence of telepathy because 'it would mean he was abandoning the fundamental notions on which his whole life had been based.'

Sinclair replied that he saw 'no reason in the world why I should take the field on behalf of the doctrine of telepathy – except my conviction that it has been proved'. Moreover, he added, 'I see no reason why Socialists are required to be ignorant of psychology.' He might also have added, had it been known at the time, that research into telepathy had been going on in the Soviet Union right from the start, thanks in large part to the enthusiasm of Maxim Gorky for it.

Another man who read a draft of *Mental Radio* was the eminent psychologist William McDougall of Harvard University and later of Duke University, where he had been appointed professor in 1927. He agreed to write an introduction to the book, but first he wanted to see Craig's telepathic powers for himself. He told her he had a picture postcard in his coat pocket, and asked if she could describe it.

She could. She said she saw a building with stone walls and narrow windows covered with green leaves. The postcard McDougall pulled out of his pocket was of an ivy-covered Oxford college building.

He then told Craig that what she had done had already decided him – he was going to Duke University in a week or two and his first action would be to set up a Department of Parapsychology.

He would have done this anyway, together with the two young assistants he had already taken on, J. B. and Louisa Rhine, but there is no doubt that the Sinclairs played an important part in the establishment of parapsychology as an academic discipline by convincing McDougall that there really was something worth studying.

At first, some of his positive experimenter effect seemed to have been passed on to the Rhines, for soon after J. B. Rhine became head of the Parapsychology Laboratory at Duke in 1934 he began to report very successful results at card guessing mainly thanks to a couple of star performers named Hubert Pearce and A. J. Linzmeyer, who scored above chance level again and again, Pearce once guessing all 25 cards correctly. Yet as the laboratory research went on – and on – the inevitable happened. The decline effect set in, critics thought up ever more ingenious explanations for the early successes, the volunteers got bored, and parapsychology seemed to have ground to a halt in a swamp of sterile statistics. However, it is worth repeating the opinion of one honest critic, statistician Burton H. Camp: 'If the Rhine investigation is to be fairly attacked, it must be on other than mathematical grounds.'

INTO THE GANZFELD

A new generation of parapsychologists decided to take an entirely different approach, and in the early 1970s three young researchers had the idea, more or less independently, of using a set-up known as the Ganzfeld (German for whole or uniform field) in order to create ideal conditions for telepathy. This is very simple: subjects' eyes are covered by special goggles or half ping-pong balls so that all they can see is a uniform light, and they listen over headphones to the 'white noise' hiss and crackle of a blank tape played at high volume. They are then given instructions similar to the ones Craig Sinclair gave herself – just relax and wait for it.

Each of the three Ganzfeld researchers – Charles Honorton and William Braud in the USA and Adrian Parker in Scotland – decided to use pictures rather than those tedious Zener cards. The sender would sit in one room and concentrate on the picture while the receiver, in another room, would say out loud whatever came to mind. This was tape-recorded in a third room by an assistant who would also make notes of the impressions and the exact times they were given.

Results were very encouraging, as they also were for the first Ganzfeld experiments carried out in England. Here is an account of a typical session in which the sender was Carl Sargent of Cambridge University, one of the (then) small handful of British parapsychologists with a PhD degree, and the receiver was me.

I had done my homework, reading Craig Sinclair's chapter on do-it-yourself telepathy, and I had practised seeing hypnagogic images until I could get them almost every time. I decided to do an experiment of my own – I would not just describe what Carl was looking at down the hall, I was actually going to see it.

And so I did. Once I was kitted out with my ping-pong ball halves and earfuls of white noise, Carl's assistant switched on a red light facing me and went next door to listen to and record every word I said over the next 35 minutes. For the first seven minutes I didn't say anything, as I knew it would take time for the brain to settle down and get used to having no (normal) sensory input. Then I said:

Ah yes, there we go. Very clear. Dark animal standing on a rock and a blue background. Mountain. Blue. Very clear, that.

The image faded. Then I saw the same rock in close-up. I could even see the cracks in it. There were no more images for several minutes, and in fact there was only one in the rest of the session, of a bare, bleak and flat landscape. At 21 minutes I announced 'I'm still getting this desolate moon landscape.' It did look like pictures I had seen of the lunar surface.

When my session ended, the assistant came in with four postcards, one of which was a duplicate of the one Carl had been looking at, although she had no idea which one. She read me everything I had said from her notes and asked me to score each statement for all four pictures, from zero for 'no resemblance' to 99 for 'very strong resemblance'.

This sounded easy, but I saw I had a problem. I seemed to have picked up bits of at least three of the pictures. One did have a blue background, another did have a flat landscape in the background, while two contained both animals and rocks. Another showed a rowing boat of the same shape as the rock I had seen, and when we added up the scores, this was the winner by a very small margin.

However, it was not the picture Carl had been looking at, which was a landscape painting in which a donkey was being led past a large rock and there was a moonlike landscape in the distance. I apologized for getting it wrong, but Carl cheered me up by saying he always had tests judged independently by a colleague who was not present, as this tended to give better results than when subjects did their own scoring. Later, the independent judge scored the landscape painting a clear winner, so I had not been a total failure after all. I had shown that, as often happens, somebody had picked up the right image but given it the wrong interpretation.

Carl gave me a copy of the notes he had made while he was concentrating on the picture, and one phrase fairly leapt off the page at me. At 21 minutes into my session, he had written 'Rather like the surface of the moon.' This is almost exactly what I had said at the same time.

Later that day we did another experiment at my suggestion, with Carl at his home in Cambridge and me at mine in London. I asked him to take any picture he liked and look at it at 11.30 p.m., when I would be in bed, which I had found was the best place to see hypnagogic images. It took longer than before to see anything at all, but I kept at it and finally saw a very clear picture of a large statue on a pedestal with a bright light shining behind it. I fumbled for the bedside light and my pencil and wrote 'Figure on pedestal. Mao. Light.'

The light was very bright, like a searchlight shining behind the dark statue, which for some reason I thought was of the then Chinese leader Mao Tse-tung. I also drew what I had seen and sent a copy of my notes and drawing to Carl the following day. He in turn passed them on, together with the picture he had been looking at plus three others, to an independent judge, who gave almost full marks to one of them – William Blake's *Glad Day*. This shows an angel standing on a pedestal-like rock with a brilliant light behind it – and it was the picture Carl had been looking at.

Having two experiences like this on the same day left me in no doubt that images can be transmitted from mind to mind even over long distances. Many other viewers have done as well as I did, some of them spectacularly well. I have seen a video clip used for one of Charles Honorton's experiments with the comments of the viewer added. It showed a spider building a web, and the viewer talked about nothing at all except spiders throughout the session. Equally impressive was the clip used by Adrian Parker with parapsychologist Kathy Dalton as receiver giving almost a blow-by-blow account of the cartoon he was watching in another room.

NO EVIDENCE?

'There is not a single parapsychological effect that can be repeatedly or reliably produced in any laboratory suitably equipped to perform and control the experiment. Not one,' wrote psychologist P. M. Churchland in his book *Matter and Consciousness* in 1984. Well, there is now. Parapsychologist Dean Radin trawled through every published Ganzfeld study carried out between 1974 and 1997 and found there had been a total of 2,549 sessions in which the overall hit rate (that is, picking the right target out of four) was 33.9 per cent where 25 per cent would be expected by chance guessing alone. The probability of this result being due to nothing but chance was one in a million billion, or 1 followed by 15 noughts.

Radin carried out a similar 'meta-analysis' of all published sheep–goat experiments in which those who accept the possibility of psi (the sheep) are predicted to perform better than everybody else (the goats). He found 73 such studies involving 37 different investigators and 4,500 subjects, the probability of the overall results being due to chance being one in a trillion. He also considered the 'file-drawer effect' whereby, critics complain, researchers report only their positive results and shove the rest into the file drawer or the bin. To bring the sheep–goat scores down to chance level, Radin calculated there would have to have been 1,726 of them.

So why, in the face of all the laboratory evidence and spontaneous case material of the kind I have mentioned in this book, do we still hear all these grumbles about 'no real evidence' for psi? I suspect that Upton Sinclair's materialist friend gave the right answer when he said he could not accept telepathy because it would mean giving up his 'fundamental notions'. Radin gives another possible answer:

> *Even though theoretical physicists have seriously discussed the possibility of mind-matter [and mind-mind] interaction, a scientific taboo about* empirically *studying such topics – referred to by Einstein as 'spooky' effects at a distance – prevails and reflects a host of underlying assumptions about the way* nature *ought to work. [His emphasis.]*[9]

There was a time not so long ago when the Sun ought to have revolved around the Earth, which ought to have been at the centre of creation as well as flat. Meteorites ought not to have fallen from the sky because they ought not to have been there in the first place. We are constantly having to change our view about how nature actually does work. It is also time, I suggest, that we change our view about how we work.

Telepathy does happen, and in this chapter I have described some of the ways it has been researched. In a later chapter I will be giving examples of how it has been put to practical use, in at least one case undoubtedly saving a life. It happens, as we have seen, not only between identical twins but also between total strangers provided they make the necessary preparations for it. Anyone can walk into a Ganzfeld laboratory and do a test in which they may succeed even though they have only just met the experimenter, and perhaps for no more than a few minutes. That is long enough to form a bond, which it seems there must be for telepathy to take place. I do not know of any case in which messages have been picked up from somebody the receiver has never met. That said, I should mention a case of what looks like telepathy by accident in which the Irish poet, painter and mystic George W. Russell, who wrote under the pseudonym AE, describes receiving a clear impression of what turned out to be an office colleague's home, which the colleague was thinking about at the time. Russell speculated that much so-called inspiration might originate from a source unknown to the receiver and so have a telepathic component.

The closer the bond, as I have said, the stronger the telepathic link, and since the identical twin bond is both the closest and the longest lasting, we should expect them to demonstrate the telepathic signal at full strength, as indeed some of them do, receiving not only images but emotions, physical impressions and, as we shall see, even apparitions. Just why some of them, probably the majority, never receive anything at all is as much a mystery as why any of them, or anybody else for that matter, receives anything by telepathy.

Many factors may be involved. The personality of the twins and the degree of their identicality seems to have an effect, as does the type of incident that gets picked up. So it would seem logical that the best telepathic impressions are picked up in cases of shock, pain, illness or crisis.

Or, of course, the ultimate crisis – death.

CHAPTER 7

HALF OF ME GONE

There is a popular belief that between twins there exists at times an affinity which surpasses the normal. The following experience of twin brothers, while both were engaged in serving their country, would seem to indicate that there are grounds for this belief.

A certain corporal, who was with his regiment at a home station, had been very anxious for some time about his twin brother who was fighting in France. He had not heard from him for some weeks, and as he had been a fairly regular correspondent, this worried him a great deal.

One night he was awakened from a deep sleep by the sound of his name being spoken: he sat up in bed and listened, but the call was not repeated.

And then, as he looked across the room, in the semi-darkness he saw quite plainly his brother sitting on his trunk, which was near the door. Too surprised to pause to reason how he could have got there, the corporal jumped quickly out of bed to greet him, but as he approached the spot the apparition had vanished. All the rest of the night he tossed and turned in his bed, for he could not sleep. He had the feeling that his brother was in danger.

Next morning he related his experience to his landlady, and also mentioned it to his mother when he wrote home. As at the time he was suffering from dyspepsia and overstrain, his friends put the vision down to 'nerves'. They were of a very different opinion, however, when a few days later the corporal received a field postcard from his brother, stating that he had been wounded at the Battle of Loos, at the very hour when he had seemed to see him sitting on the box in his room.[1]

As so often, this case, which was published in 1919, was not reported in as much detail as we would like. The corporal is not named, and we are not told how the author got hold of the story. It is rather surprising that the brother mentioned the exact time he was wounded, if indeed he did. If he did not, how did the author know it was 'at the very hour'? This is a second-hand account of a kind all too easy to dismiss.

I am not dismissing it for several reasons. One is that it was reported by a highly experienced and reputable researcher, Hereward Carrington, who was known for his skill at detecting fraud and trickery. He must have believed the story or he would not have published it. Another reason is that it is very similar to another case that I will mention here in which the well-known witness was named. It is also good evidence for a 'popular belief' in a special twin connection as early as 1919 when there was very little in print about it. It is a pity that Carrington, author of several books on psychical research, does not seem to have enquired further into it.

What really intrigues me about this case is the fact that the sighting, so typical of those known as deathbed apparitions in which somebody who is dying puts in a brief farewell appearance to a loved one, was of a man who was still alive. He seems to have communicated in three ways: first waking his brother by calling his name, then becoming visible, and finally conveying the impression, which turned out to be correct, that he was not dead but only 'in danger'.

Carrington's 1919 case has much in common with a more recent one reported by author Ruth Montgomery,[2] who presumably heard it from the source, the distinguished American diplomat Loy Henderson, who had served as his country's ambassador in Iran and India.

He had an identical twin brother Roy, with whom he had a very close affinity. When they were young 'to the annoyance of their family, they often communicated with each other by means of an isolated word, rather than needing to complete a sentence.'

Twins, it seems, often do this, sometimes apparently inventing their own private language. An amusing example of this is given by twin expert Dr Carol Cooper in which a mother of one-year-olds described to her what happened one day when she took the boys out to the shops:

> *I was in a bookshop with Alex and Kim facing each other in their pram. Alex made a few noises, Kim gurgled fluently in reply as if telling a joke and they were off in fits of giggles. It brought business in the shop to a standstill as people gawped.*[3]

Another mother has described to me hearing the same kind of twinspeak from her little girls at an age when they were far from fluent in English. They could keep it up for hours, she told me, and really seemed to be communicating something. There is possible evidence for telepathy here, yet it is not easy to extract useful information from a subject who can only gurgle!

Dr Cooper mentions in passing that a number of twins have told her that they believe they can read each other's minds, but gives no examples. Yet another research opportunity missed.

If the Henderson twins' private language indicated no more than childish fun and games, the distressing experience that Loy went through as a young man is harder to dismiss. In 1920, Roy was a student at Harvard and Loy was serving with a Red Cross unit in Estonia, some 5,000 miles away. One evening as he lay in a hospital bed during a typhus epidemic, he:

> *had a sudden feeling that he was dying. At that instant his twin brother appeared to him, and Loy says of the eerie episode: 'I was telling him goodbye. Both of us spoke of our deep distress at being separated from each other by death. Then he vanished.'*

Two of Loy's colleagues had died of typhus, so he had good reason to be in fear of his own life as he lay in his hospital bed. Yet it was found that he did not have the disease after all and he was able to return to his unit. One evening he was having a bath when an officer called through the door to say he had a telegram for him. Loy immediately replied that he was sure it brought news of his brother's death. His colleague offered to read it for him, and Loy told him to go ahead. Then:

> *there was a blank silence beyond the door. The cable stated that Roy had died of an infection after having a tooth extracted. His death occurred at the same time as my vision.*

It also must have come as a complete surprise. Whereas the soldier in Carrington's case knew his brother was on active service and was quite likely to be killed or wounded, as so many thousands were in the First World War, Roy Henderson's death can hardly have been expected. Yet once again a twin reports actually seeing his brother although he must have known that he could not possibly be where he seemed to be.

Loy's confusion when he thought he and not his twin was dying reminds us of the Rev. Wilson's similar experience, which I described in Chapter 2. It seems that the twin connection can be so close that there are times when twins cannot be sure which are their feelings and which are the other's. How such an affinity can extend over thousands of miles, conveying wholly unpredictable and specific sensations as well as vague impressions and even recognizable images, can be accounted for only in terms of an order of reality most of us have not yet explored, although fortunately some of us have as I will describe later.

More evidence for a warning of a twin's death comes from a source whose honesty seems beyond question: the Rev. Christopher Chavasse, the first Master of St Peter's College, Oxford, who later became Bishop of Rochester. His biographer Canon Selwyn

Gummer, who knew him well, describes how he and his twin brother Noel:

> *became one in mind and spirit, even to anticipating each other's wishes and sharing one another's pain, an experience which persisted until death separated them.*

The headmaster of their school described an incident very similar to others I have mentioned (and many more I have no room to mention):

> *Noel had toothache and Christopher was found at the same time weeping with pain in another part of the school, and quite ignorant of his twin's distress or the cause of his personal suffering.*

Death was to separate the Chavasse twins early. Both joined the army and fought in the First World War, Christopher being wounded and losing a leg, and Noel dying in action on another part of the front.

Many years later, Christopher wrote a letter of condolence to one of his parishioners who had lost a twin sister. He knew just how she felt:

> *I think my experience has been rather what I went through when I lost my leg. My loss of my twin was like amputation – I felt half of me gone, for we were extremely close, so that I knew (I have proof of this) when he died, though he was eighty miles away at the battle-front, and the news did not reach me till he had been dead a week.*[4]

It would be interesting to know what that proof was, but we can hardly imagine a bishop telling a lie on an occasion like this. As for that feeling of 'half of me gone', another example of it came to light after the death of the novelist Thornton Wilder, who wrote very sensitively about a pair of twins, one of whom is killed, in one of his most popular novels. While editing his journals, his sister Isabel Wilder came across a letter written to him by a woman who had lost her twin, complaining that neither her husband nor her grown-up children seemed to understand the extent of her grief. 'But from what you write about twins in *The Bridge of San Luis Rey*,' she wrote, 'I know you do. How do you know?'

The answer, Isabel Wilder explained, was quite simple. Thornton was a twin himself.

Like most twins the babies were premature and very frail. Thornton came first. The second child, perfectly formed and identical, was stillborn. Thornton missed this lost companion all his life.[5]

A somewhat different reaction to the death of a twin was poignantly described by Norris McWhirter, whom I mentioned at the beginning of this book. He was on his way home after performing the unimaginably harrowing duty of identifying his murdered twin's body:

As I was being driven back through the roadblock in a policeman's car, with my head under a blanket, I felt that I was about to be reborn – not as half a person but as a double person.[6]

As I have said, he does not mention having been aware of his brother's shooting at the time, and there is no mention of any kind of telepathic link anywhere in his biography of his brother apart from the comment 'No more would we be able to share our thoughts', which could mean no more than that they enjoyed discussing things, just like any other pair of friends or relatives.

The murder had taken place early in the evening, as Norris

McWhirter was just about to leave his home 30 miles away with his wife and son Alasdair, then aged 12. How I came to learn what happened next is quite a story in itself. In 1999 a friend called me to ask if I was interested in a quick writing assignment and gave the phone number and name of the publisher – Alasdair McWhirter. Yes, I was told, he was Norris's son.

We arranged a meeting, and Alasdair asked me to bring along something I had written recently. As luck, or maybe angel guardianship, would have it, the last thing I had published was an article about twin telepathy, which opened with the quotation from *The Corsican Brothers* I mentioned in Chapter 2 in which the hero describes how he reacted to his brother's distant death.

The coffee arrived; I handed Alasdair the journal. Almost as soon as he had opened it and begun to read, I nearly dropped my cup.

'That's exactly what my father did,' he said. I had hardly said a word to him at that stage other than the usual greetings and had no intention of mentioning such a delicate subject as his uncle's murder on our first meeting, though I had hoped to bring it up when I got to know him better. He went on, without any prompting or questioning from me:

We were getting ready to go to my sister's school play, and I was standing in the drawing room with my father. Suddenly, for no apparent reason, he slumped down into a chair. He looked dazed. I was terrified and thought he had suffered a heart attack. A few minutes later he recovered, the phone rang, and it was the police.

Later, I told Alasdair that I had tried to contact his father in the early 1980s via the husband of a friend, who worked for him and knew him well. After a long delay I was told that the man had been unable to learn anything about how Norris had reacted, if at all, though it was not quite clear if he had actually asked him directly. By then, my friend's husband was her ex-husband, and I could not pursue the matter. I did not feel inclined to write to somebody I did not know and ask 'Very briefly, how did you feel when your brother was shot?'

Alasdair told me that even if his father had been asked, he would have replied that he had no memory at all of how he had reacted, having wiped the incident from his mind. Once again, a close relative provided better evidence of the kind I was looking for than the twin concerned could have given me. Such are the roundabout ways in which important pieces of evidence can turn up quite unexpectedly when they might have gone unreported for ever. This episode reinforced my belief that there is far more evidence for the twin connection than will ever be made public, and I was thinking of attempting a large-scale survey, which would have been both expensive and time-consuming when I found to my delight that this had already been done.

THE ROSAMBEAU SURVEY

Some idea of how much evidence there is for a twin connection was given by Mary Rosambeau. In 1987 she made public appeals in several newspapers and magazines, as a result of which she was able to get completed questionnaires from 600 twins or parents of twins. These included questions on all aspects of twinhood, and the two that concern us here were:

1. Have you or your twin(s) had any experience which might be explained as being able to read each other's minds? If so, what?
2. Have you ever been surprised by both of you having the same illness or pain at the same time?

A total of 183 people, or just over 30 per cent, replied yes to at least one of these questions. This is almost the same percentage that Galton found to have 'extremely close resemblance' and the Toronto team reckoned to be telepathy-prone. Mary Rosambeau soon noticed that the accounts she was sent fell into six clearly recognizable categories, which she listed as follows:

1. Anticipation of imminent contact, or knowing when the twin is about to make a telephone call. This is suggestive of telepathy, but not proof of it.
2. Simultaneous expression of identical speech or thought – twins saying the same thing at the same time, one singing a tune the other was thinking of, and, as one twin put it, 'We often answer a question that the other has not yet asked.' This, especially the last example, is rather more suggestive of telepathy.
3. Simultaneous identical written work. I have already given examples of this, and Mary Rosambeau collected several more. This is clearly a common phenomenon and a borderline one that can be seen as the normal result of two identical minds facing the same problem after doing the same homework. However, let us not forget Newman's twins who claimed to have read half the set books each, and the boy who refused to start writing until his distant twin was ready.

Scientists talk about Type A and Type B errors – either claiming something to be true which is false, or the other way round – claiming something to be false which is true. It is all too easy to make both errors when deciding if twin telepathy exists. In the case of simultaneous writing we can avoid both types of error by suggesting, as I believe, that this shows a combination of genetics and telepathy at work.
4. Simultaneous expression of identical taste. This is another borderline one, involving buying the same clothes, presents, wallpaper or whatever. Mary Rosambeau correctly points out that, 'society creates an atmosphere in which twins and their associates around them are always keen to notch up another score on the side of ESP' – a typical Type B error. However, it may be another Type B error to assume that this explains away all examples of twin coincidence.
5. Just knowing. Again and again, twins report that they 'just

knew' something, invariably that something was wrong. Here, the evidence for telepathy is much stronger. Again and again, twins reported, 'I felt something was wrong', 'I felt very uneasy', 'I was overcome with misery' and so on. One woman reported, 'If I feel depressed for no reason at all, I wonder if it's Sandra's fault, and sure enough the phone will ring and she's in trouble.' Another described how she was waiting for a bus to take her to college, her twin having taken the previous one, 'when I was overcome with misery'. She cried in the bus all the way to college, where she found her sister had fallen down some stairs and hurt herself badly. Curiously, she felt no physical pain, just sudden distress.

6. Sympathetic pain. This must be the most suggestive of telepathy of all, at least when the pain results from something which cannot be predicted. It may be quite normal if two twins get a toothache together, but how do we account for the case of the woman who received a phone call from her sister in Canada begging her to have her teeth checked because she had an awful toothache although her dentist had x-rayed her teeth and found nothing wrong with them? Teeth do not ache for no reason.

One twin after another reported shared or transferred pain when one of them broke a bone, or was burned, cut or slapped and the other one felt it. One mother described how one of her babies cut himself and did not cry, yet the other twin yelled and screamed as if in agony. Sometimes, as in the case of the Spanish twins I mentioned in Chapter 4, there was visible evidence for shared pain. A woman described how, on a visit to her twin sister, she had shown her a large bruise that had appeared on her leg. She had no idea what might have caused it. 'She then showed me her same leg with an identical bruise – she had trapped hers in a car door.'

Shock as well as pain can be shared, and I gave an example of this earlier with the case of the American student who told me how she woke up in alarm when a bomb had gone off outside her sister's home, but without hurting her. One of Mary Rosambeau's informants told her how both her twin daughters had phoned her for a chat one day, one right after the other. The first told her about a nightmare she had just had in which someone was shining a bright light in her face, as if she was being interrogated. The second happened to mention that she had just had a shock – her roommate had come back in the middle of the night and had thoughtlessly switched on the ceiling light.[7]

This important survey, almost certainly the largest of its kind on record, contained surprises. One was that some twins did not seem to know if they were telepathy-prone or not. One pair even claimed that they often knew what the other was thinking. 'But it was not ESP.' They did not say what they thought it was. Another commented 'I don't think I would know where shared experience stopped and ESP began.' Another described how 'sometimes I lie there thinking, am I getting a message or is it just indigestion?'

Another surprise was the high incidence of telepathy between non-identicals, and it may be thought that I am putting too much emphasis on the identicals in this book. I will go into this question later, when all my evidence has been presented.

Mary Rosambeau has contributed more to the study of the twin connection than all the researchers mentioned in previous chapters put together. Her survey fully confirms my earlier discovery that examples of twin-connections fell into clearly recognizable categories that cover a spectrum from almost certainly normal to almost certainly not normal.

An even larger survey, though not solely concerned with twins, was carried out by Dr Shari Cohn of the School of Scottish Studies at the University of Edinburgh. She was mainly interested in the question of whether telepathy and clairvoyance, or what the Scots call 'second sight' has a hereditary component, but she noticed that after analysing more than 1,000 cases, reports of telepathy were

three times as common from twins as they were from non-twins. [8]
Further, though qualified, support for this finding was provided
by Evelyn R. Bohm, who chose for her PhD thesis at Columbia
University Teachers College the subject of 'nonverbal
communication between individuals who share a close emotional
bond'.[9] I have unfortunately been able to see only the author's
summary of this, and although it gives no figures, it makes
tantalizing reading. Using GSR (galvanic skin response)
equipment, she claimed to have shown that 'shared states' of pain,
feelings or emotions could be instrumentally recorded, which is
just what the much-maligned Duane and Behrendt had claimed
back in the Sixties.

She divided her subjects into three groups: 'psychics', identical
twins and 'generally close dyads' such as roommates or non-twin
relatives. She found the twins did better than the non-twins, but
the psychics did best of all. This suggests that there is more than
one cause for telepathy-proneness, which only makes the whole
subject more complicated to research than it already was.

I have to apologize for bombarding readers with yet more case
histories in the following chapter. However, like any good
prosecuting attorney I want to present the best evidence I can to
enable them to reach a fair verdict (by which I mean of course to
agree with me!) and to explain why it is taking so long for the
evidence to become accepted.

CHAPTER 8

SOMETHING FROM SOMEWHERE

While carrying out research many years ago into the history of medical hypnotism, I could not help noticing how often in the past it had become popular, brought about some spectacular cures of supposedly incurable diseases, and then almost disappeared only to reappear, produce more miracle cures and then vanish again, and so on right up to the present day. I suspect the taboo factor has been at work here, as Catherine Crowe had complained back in 1848.

So it has been with research into the twin connection, which even in January 2000 was still being treated by the media as if it either did not exist or had just been discovered for the first time. In that month, a whole page of Britain's top-selling newspaper was devoted to a story about the misfortunes of 10-year-old identical twins Natalie and Zara Haywood from County Durham.[1] And a remarkable story it was.

They were clearly a pair of mirror twins. One was left-handed, the other right-handed, and they parted their hair on different sides. Their mother recalled that when they were babies one would always go to sleep lying on her left side and the other on her right, as they were still doing after ten years. Synchronized sleeping!

'If I tried to move them,' she said, 'they'd just roll back into their original positions.' When they were asleep, they looked like 'two halves of the same coin'. This I found a particularly interesting comment, for reasons that will become clear later.

As they grew up, the girls invariably caught the same diseases and infections at the same time, as we would expect. Less predictable and less easy to explain were the series of simultaneous accidents. Both fell off their bicycles within minutes of each other, one cutting herself on the left leg, the other on her right. Both pulled muscles in their legs, again one left and the other right, while swimming in the same pool at almost exactly the same time. Both broke their arms (one left, one right, of course) in roller-skating accidents within half an hour of each other. Their mother had become resigned to the fact that 'if one of them has a mishap I'll be nursing the mirror injury in the other a few minutes later'. This was all beginning to look like more than carelessness.

Under the headline 'Doc: It's Just Coincidence', the paper's medical adviser Dr Hilary Jones came up with this expert opinion:

The way that the twins' accidents mirror each other is very unusual, but it's probably due to sheer coincidence and nothing else. In cases like this parents tend to concentrate on events which fit into a pattern and conveniently forget things that don't.

He offered no evidence to support this non-explanation, and as I have said he could not have because there is no sign of any. The writer of the article rang me a few days before it was published, saying that she had been told that I was the country's leading expert on twin telepathy, to which I replied that as far as I knew I was the only one. She then told me about the Haywood twins' adventures, read me the doctor's comments and asked for my reaction, which I duly gave. It must have been considered unprintable, even by British Sunday tabloid standards, because the box where it could have appeared was filled with an advertisement. What I said, more or less, was:

For a start, twin accidents are not unusual but quite usual. I have several accounts of similar ones. What is highly unusual is for the same pair to have so many of them. Banging on about 'sheer coincidence' explains nothing and just postpones serious investigation.

Dr Jones did concede that, 'We hear a lot about twins connecting mentally with one another, and although it has not been medically proven, in some cases it might be true.' He used almost the same words as some of the twin experts I have already mentioned. Again, there seems to be a general awareness that there is some special twin connection, but little inclination, if any, to look into it. It is taboo.

THE RESEARCH GAME

Why should this be? I suggest that the reason is the same as it is for the lack of serious research into the potential and limitations of hypnosis. This was amusingly spelled out by London hypnotherapist Dr Ashley Conway in a 1988 article in which he described what had happened when a post-graduate student at Bristol University suggested to his professor that there seemed to be a need for some quality research into hypnosis.

'I would never allow it in my department,' replied the prof.

'Why not?' the student asked.

'Because hypnosis is not a respectable field for research.' Why not? 'Because it has no serious published literature.' And why would that be? 'Because nobody has done the research.' Why haven't they? 'Because hypnosis is not a respectable field for research.'[2]

This runaround was part of what Dr Conway calls the Research Game, one of the rules of which is 'Do not research an entirely new field.'

There is a well-known piece of scientific equipment known as Occam's razor, named after the 14th-century philosopher William of Occam (or Ockham) who laid down the sensible law that 'entities should not be posited without necessity'. This means that the simplest explanation for anything is usually the best, and that unknown phenomena should be explained in terms of what is known.

Fair enough. Yet Occam's imaginary razor can be overwielded. To dismiss all twin connections as 'sheer coincidence and nothing else' overlooks the question of why twins experience more of them than anybody else, as they undoubtedly do. Is there a single case on record of, say, a brother and non-twin sister breaking their legs at the same time miles apart, or of one of them feeling a bang on the head when the other one is banged on the head? There are cases of such sympathetic reaction between mothers and small children and between dogs and their owners, but they are the exceptions and not the rule.

Just how common twin coincidences were became evident when I was able to get access to a large collection of videotapes that included 20 programmes about twins and other multiple births. These ranged from a three-part BBC series presented by the distinguished medical researcher Lord Winston[3] and a documentary on the work of the Minnesota team to a number of chat shows hosted by the likes of Esther Rantzen, Oprah Winfrey, Robert Kilroy-Silk and Vanessa Feltz.[4]

To my surprise, the chat shows did a much more useful job than any of the 'serious' programmes. In the programme I mentioned in Chapter 1 the 'daft question' of telepathy was raised just once and instantly dismissed, none of several other twin pairs in the programme being asked it. In the Minnesota film there was a hasty mention about two women who bought similar dresses, while in a lengthy documentary on the Dionne quintuplets (at least two of whom were probably identical, though we were not told if they were) it was not mentioned at all.

Lord Winston gave the impression of setting out to prove that twins are not telepathic at all. A well-known technique used by players of the Research Game is to do what looks like a proper experiment, but has in fact been designed to prove what you want to prove, and he gave a splendid example of it. Just one pair of twins was taken to the impressive-looking laboratory at the University of Hertfordshire, one of the very few in Britain to receive funding for parapsychological research, and were given a Ganzfeld test in which one twin was asked to choose a picture out of a set of four and transmit it to her sister in another room. She was then asked to do the same with a picture selected for her by the experimenter, Dr Richard Wiseman (a very high profile sceptic). It was not clear how many times the experiment was repeated – television has no time for such trivial details.

The receiving twin was shown a set of four pictures after each test and asked to pick the one her sister had been looking at. When the sender had chosen her own pictures, the receiver guessed them at well above chance level, but when the picture had been chosen for her, results were exactly at chance. This was taken as proof of 'thought concordance' and disproof of telepathy. Lord Winston did not quite say, 'There you are, nothing in it', yet this was the clear message, on the basis of a brief experiment involving just one pair of twins that no serious journal would have dreamed of publishing.

A SURPRISE IN A TELEVISION STUDIO

At the other extreme, a mind-numbingly awful show hosted by Ricki Lake assembled a whole studio full of triplets and included an 'experiment' in which all three members of a set were asked to name their favourite pop and film stars. Not surprisingly, many of the sets shared the same preferences, and although some did not, this was hailed as shattering proof that triplets are telepathic.

The chat shows hosted by Esther Rantzen, Robert Kilroy-Silk and Oprah Winfrey did a much better job by letting us hear from the twins themselves the kind of experiences they have had. Naturally, these were all what sceptics patronizingly call 'self-reported' or 'anecdotal', implying that they cannot possibly be taken seriously (unlike evidence in courts of law, which is often anecdotal and self-reported). Yet they were impressive by their consistency.

It was mostly the familiar stuff – pain felt at a distance when a twin was having a baby, an operation or a tooth pulled out. There was dramatic support for my imaginary bang on the head experiment from twins who actually had been hit on the head, beaten up in the middle of the night, or in one tragic case electrocuted. There were also persuasive and often moving accounts from separated and reunited twins of the 'void', the 'deep hole that bothered me', or the 'feeling of something missing' they had experienced during their separation.

I was contacted by the *Kilroy* programme and asked to take part as the expert I seemed to have become on the strength of just two short articles for a twin association magazine. I was unable to accept, but asked the producer if he could persuade the host to do an experiment for me by asking a whole studio full of twins how many of them thought they had experience of telepathy. I predicted that about a third of them would have had, the majority of them women.

So they had and so they were. Halfway through the 50-minute programme the host asked a pair of young women to describe their experiences, and the whole of the rest of the time was devoted to similar accounts, nearly all of them from women, which suggests that while women may not experience any more telepathy than men do, they are more willing to talk about it in front of a television camera.

Of all the 20 videos I sat through, one was in a class of its own, since it showed a successful experiment of considerable scientific value being conducted in front of a large audience. This was one of the programmes in the 1997 series *The Paranormal World of Paul McKenna* for Carlton TV, and I am proud of the fact that the experiment was my idea.[5]

I was hired as a consultant at the pre-production stage of the series, and asked to come up with suggestions for suitable material, and one of my first was for a twin experiment of some kind. Paul

McKenna promptly announced, 'Yes, we'll do it,' and I managed to persuade the producer to look for the right kind of twins as described by the Toronto researchers. They had to be extraverts, absolutely identical, preferably female, and supersheep (firm believers in telepathy).

In due course, the production team rounded up four pairs who met these requirements, and decided to do a trial run before filming began in order to select the one most likely to perform on cue. One of each pair was chosen to be the sender, seated in a comfortable chair, and just asked to relax while the other, the receiver, was taken to a room well out of earshot and wired up to a multi-channel polygraph under the supervision of lie-detector expert Jeremy Barrett. Neither twin had any idea what was going to happen. They were just told that some unspecified and harmless experiment was being done.

When the senders had been relaxing for 10 minutes or so they were given quite a surprise, when a very loud alarm that had been fitted to the back of the chair went off within inches of their ears. The idea was to give them a shock without doing any physical damage, as it certainly did, and see if anything showed up on Mr Barrett's chart paper. There was evidence that it did indeed for three of the four sets of twins, and the best evidence was produced by two very lively teenagers, Evelyn and Elaine Dove, so they were chosen to take part in the studio programme.

'Would you say that you have a psychic bond or psychic link between yourselves?' Paul McKenna asked them when they had bounded on to the stage.

'Yes,' one of them replied at once. 'It's something that cannot be explained – but things just happen.'

'What kind of things happen?'

'Well, there was one occasion when I was in hospital after an operation, and I was in a lot of pain, and my sister came next day and said, "I didn't sleep last night – you were in a lot of pain, weren't you?"'

'That's right.' This was not a very good start – she might have just been worried, knowing that her sister was recovering from an operation and was quite likely to be in pain. Yet there was better to come.

Evelyn was taken out of the studio to a room with two soundproof doors separating it from the studio, and wired up to the polygraph by Jeremy Barrett while Elaine sat on the studio stage in front of a large pyramid put together by the special-effects team. Paul McKenna then gave her some ingenious misdirection:

'We're just going to see if your thoughts can be transferred to your sister,' he said soothingly, 'so just relax, think about something that's really nice and relaxing for a moment, maybe a time you went on holiday, something like that, so just relax, do that now, relax deeply, really relax…'

You are not allowed to show a hypnotic induction on British television because, I am told, of an incident in the early days when half the country was apparently put to sleep by a hypnotist, but this came close to being one. Paul McKenna had cleverly implied that just Elaine's thoughts were going to be recorded down the hall somehow or other. No alarms on the back of the chair this time.

There was indeed no alarm on the back of the chair. However, shortly after Elaine seemed to have gone into a light trance the pyramid a few feet in front of her exploded with a tremendous bang, emitting clouds of coloured smoke and sparks and giving both Elaine and the audience quite a shock.

Paul McKenna then called Mr Barrett and asked him to give his earphones to Evelyn. 'Were you aware of anything going on?' he asked her.

She seemed to have been, but found it hard to put into words. 'I could just feel – it's very hard to explain, but the fact that she was – we were both trying to relax, and she was very nervous, but as soon as it finished I opened my eyes and knew she was OK.'

'Does that mean you somehow knew exactly how she was feeling?' Paul McKenna continued.

'Yes.' This was a leading question, and Evelyn's reply was far from proof of telepathy. It was merely a rather incoherent account of what she could well have guessed: that Elaine was feeling a bit nervous in front of a large audience and several million viewers. Yet the best was still to come.

When the polygraph chart was played back on a split screen so that both twins could be seen side by side, Evelyn's brain waves, blood pressure and galvanic skin response could be seen jogging smoothly along the chart paper until the moment of the explosion, at which there were some very large fluctuations, one pen nearly going off the chart. Paul McKenna asked Mr Barrett who, like Evelyn, had no idea what had been going on in the studio, what he made of this.

'Well,' he replied, 'Evelyn certainly picked up something from somewhere.' He confirmed that she had not been given any kind of stimulus during the experiment, but had just been asked to relax and think about her sister. 'There certainly was something coming,' Mr Barrett added, 'and it looks to me like shock or surprise.' It is interesting that despite her visible reactions, Evelyn had no conscious awareness of any shock. Without the polygraph chart this experiment would have been worthless.

Now, having just told Lord Winston off for implying that twins are not telepathic on the basis of a single brief experiment, I am not going to make the same mistake and claim that Paul McKenna and the Dove sisters proved that they are. They merely provided more evidence to support the claims of Duane and Behrendt, and of Aristide Esser, that community of sensation between twins can be recorded instrumentally.

The experiment needs to be repeated many times before we can claim to have proved anything, and as I will describe later a similar experiment had in fact been done three years earlier although I did not know about it at the time. It requires no more than a standard piece of equipment that every university in the country should have, and some well-selected twins.

Taboos and Tabooism

There are several large twin registers in addition to the Minnesota one, notably in Italy, Japan and Sweden, while London's St Thomas's Hospital has several thousand pairs on its books. There, I was told, they are mainly interested in monitoring twins' physical processes in order to learn more about genetic origins of disease. However, they also found time to test 127 pairs of twins for similarity in their sense of humour, which seems to add little of value to the sum of human knowledge. I asked a member of the twin unit if it might be possible to use their register to seek volunteers for experiments in what I called, carefully avoiding the T word, 'physiological correlates of empathy'.

'What's that?' I was asked.

'Oh, er, you know, what some people call telepathy,' I replied. I could think of no other word for it, and my mention of it had just the effect I didn't want. The unit, I was told sternly, was not interested in 'spooky stuff'. I should have known – telepathy is taboo.

I made my excuses and left.

The word taboo came into the English language in 1777 when Captain James Cook noted in his diary that the inhabitants of the Friendly Islands used the word, as an adjective, to mean something that was 'under prohibition, forbidden or set apart'. It is now used, as noun or adjective, to mean something that is simply not to be mentioned or even allowed to exist. There is a powerful and insidious taboo against what sceptics call 'the paranormal', which covers everything from telepathy and clairvoyance to spoon-bending, flying saucers, alien abductions, crop circles, astrology, the Loch Ness monster and the Abominable Snowperson.

The word paranormal, as an adjective, simply means 'beyond the range of normal experience or scientific explanation'. It has also become a noun used to denote anything that is inexplicable in terms of science as presently understood. Reactions to it can be quite extreme, as this piece of somewhat unscientific language from an article by Professor Richard Dawkins indicates:

The paranormal is bunk. Those who try to sell it to us are fakes and charlatans. And some of them have grown rich and fat by taking us for a ride.[6]

Dawkins and his fellow Oxford academic Professor Peter Atkins are prominent members of the sanctimoniously entitled Committee for the Public Understanding of Science (COPUS), better known to some as the Committee for the Proclamation of Unassailable Truth (COPOUT). In an interview in which he was asked to explain his attitude to parapsychology, Atkins has cheerfully admitted, 'Yes, I admit that I am prejudiced, if you like I am a bigot and I have my mind closed to this kind of research.' He explained why:

It's just a waste of time. Serious scientists have got real things to think about – we don't have time to waste on claims which we know both in our hearts and heads must be nonsense at root... I think there is no known effect that cannot be explained by conventional science.[7]

Even discussion of taboo seems to have become taboo, but one critic who has taken the bull by the horns and given it a ferocious shaking is science writer Richard Milton. What he calls 'tabooism' is, he says, essentially, 'derision and rejection by scientists (and non-scientists) of those new discoveries or new inventions that cannot be fitted into the existing framework of knowledge'. He cites some of the classic cases of tabooism – the French Academy of Science's refusal to admit the existence of meteorites, the insistence on the impossibility of powered flight even after the Wright brothers had taken off in full view of passing cars and trains, and the rejection of Edison's electric light, partly because he was an amateur outsider. Milton continues:

In its more subtle form, the taboo reaction draws a circle around a subject and places it 'out of bounds' to any form of rational analysis or investigation. In doing so, science often puts up what appears to be a well-considered, fundamental objection, which on closer analysis turns out to be no more than the unreflecting prejudices of a maiden aunt who feels uncomfortable about the idea of mixed bathing.

The real damage done by tabooism, he says, is that it has a 'cumulative and permanent discriminatory effect', and he refers to the 'intellectual Devil's Island where convicted concepts are sent', explaining:

Any idea that is ideologically suspect or counter to the current paradigm is permanently dismissed, and the very fact of its rejection forms the basis of its rejection on all future occasions.[8]

By another of those curious coincidences, while I was writing the final draft of this chapter there was an explosion of tabooism in the media, directed against Professor Brian Josephson, winner of the 1973 Nobel Prize for physics. The Royal Mail had invited six British laureates to write a short piece about their fields for a brochure to accompany a special issue of stamps commemorating the centenary of the first awards. Josephson wrote a concise summary of quantum theory, noting that this led to 'capturing in mathematical form a mysterious, elusive world containing "spooky effects at a distance" [as Einstein called them] real enough to lead to inventions such as the laser and the transistor.' So far so good. Yet his conclusion opened up a sizeable can of worms:

Quantum theory is now being combined with theories of information and computation. These developments may lead to an explanation of processes still not understood within conventional science, such as telepathy – an area in which Britain is at the forefront of research.[9]

The very idea that quantum theory might go some way towards explaining telepathy – which, as I will show, it might – was too much for some. 'It's a subject people get quite emotional about,' said Josephson in the understatement of the week. 'The reaction I have received has been more hostile than I expected.'

The most hostile critic was yet another sceptical Oxford professor, David Deutsch. 'Telepathy simply does not exist,' he shrieked. 'The Royal Mail has let itself be hoodwinked into supporting ideas that are complete nonsense.' Josephson might well have repeated the remark attributed to Newton in a similar context – 'Sir, I have studied the subject and you haven't' – but instead he pointed out, correctly, that 'there is a lot of evidence to support the existence of telepathy', and that the concept of mind being linked to matter was 'not a crazy idea' but 'absolutely standard physics'. He added that 'papers on the subject are being rejected, quite unfairly'. The Research Game was still being played in 2001, as vigorously as ever.

There is indeed much nonsensical bunk around, some of it dangerous bunk that fully deserves to be debunked. However the fact that telepathy cannot yet be explained, and so is still in the paranormal category, does not make it bunk. The same could be said about something the existence of which cannot be denied – gravity.

Pioneer of 'real' science though he was, Newton was also what we would today call a creationist, an extreme fundamentalist Christian convinced that God had made the world in six days (the first of which, he pointed out, was by definition of infinite length!). He regarded gravity as 'a perpetual miracle', and when his fellow mathematician Gottfried von Leibniz told him off for using such unscientific language, he retorted:

By what efficient cause these tractions [such as gravity] are performed, I do not here enquire. For we ought to learn first from the phenomena of nature what bodies mutually attract each other, and what are the laws and properties of that attraction, before we enquire by what efficient cause it is performed.[10]

He might almost have been writing about telepathy, which seems to involve the mutual attraction of two minds, and if we want to learn more about it, as experienced by non-twins as well as by twins, we should take a look at some of the best evidence for it before we look for those efficient causes, which I will be doing in the final chapter.

Now fasten your seat belts. We are about to enter a new order of reality.

CHAPTER 9

THE VIVID CONDITIONS

THE PSYCHIC CONTINUUM

The Rt. Hon. Sir Auckland Geddes was undoubtedly one of the great and the good of his day. A doctor of both medicine and law, he became a Member of Parliament in 1917, eventually holding two ministerial posts as well as a seat on the Privy Council. Later, he served as British Ambassador to the USA, and was also chairman for 22 years of the blue-chip Rio Tinto Company.

In 1935, when he was in his mid-fifties, he had a very strange experience that he described at a meeting of the Royal Medical Society in Edinburgh as one of 'a man who passed into the very portals of death and was brought back to life'. It is one of the earliest cases we have of what is now known as a near-death experience.

One evening, he had been smitten with a severe attack of gastroenteritis. It kept him awake all night, and by morning 'pulse and respirations became quite impossible to count'. He continued:

I wanted to ring for assistance, but found I could not, and so quite placidly gave up the attempt. I realised I was very ill, and very quickly reviewed my whole financial position. Thereafter at no time did my consciousness appear to me to be in any way dimmed, but I suddenly realised that my consciousness was separating from another consciousness which was also me.[1]

One of these seemed to remain firmly attached to his body, although slowly disintegrating into individual components

121

attached to 'head, heart and viscera'. The other one seemed to have left the body altogether, and this is where the story becomes really interesting:

> *Gradually I realised that I could see, not only my body and the bed in which it was, but everything in the whole house and garden, and then I realised that I was seeing not only 'things' at home but in London and Scotland, in fact wherever my attention was directed... and the explanation I received, from what source I do not know but which I found myself calling to myself my Mentor, was that I was free in a time-dimension of space, wherein 'now' was in some way equivalent to 'here' in the ordinary three-dimensional space of everyday life.*

Then he began to recognize acquaintances, each of them surrounded by a 'psychic condensation' of various colours. Somehow he became aware of 'a psychic stream flowing with life through time' and that 'all our brains are just organs projecting as it were from the three-dimensional universe into the psychic stream'. This was all very strange, and he must have found it hard to describe. Yet at the same time he was still aware of what was going on in real life:

> *Just when I began to grasp all these [condensations] I saw 'A' enter the bedroom; I realised she got a terrible shock and I saw her hurry to the telephone. I saw my doctor leave his patients and come very quickly, and heard him say, or saw him think, 'He is nearly gone.' I heard him quite clearly speaking to me on the bed, but I was not in touch with my body and could not answer.*

An injection of camphor soon brought him back to it, rather to his disappointment, because 'I was so interested and just beginning to understand where I was and what I was "seeing".' The experience made a profound and lasting impression on him. 'Of one thing only can we be quite sure,' he told his audience, 'it is not a fake. Without certainty of this, I would not have brought it to your notice.'

He had a similar experience of what he called the 'thanatoid state' 10 years later following a major haemorrhage, describing it as 'substantially a repetition' of the first; and yet another towards the end of his life, when he had gone blind. This one was different – he could not see anything terrestrial, yet his ability to see 'the shining iridescence of the psychic stream' was unimpaired. He also had an intriguing exchange with his 'Mentor', asking at one point 'What is this, Mentor?' only to be told, 'There is no "Mentor". You yourself created him as a device to explain your own understandings.' I confess I am not sure what to make of that.

'It is surprising to note,' he recalled in 1952, 'that the memory of these experiences, dreams, visions or whatever they were, has shown no tendency to fade or to grow or to rationalise itself.'

His account of them is of exceptional interest, coming as it does from a professor of medicine. It was dictated soon after the event and although we have no independent testimony it seems unthinkable that Lord Geddes (as he became) wrote anything other than the truth in his memoirs. A notable feature of his experiences was that he seemed to be in two realities at once. Part of him remained sufficiently conscious to see his nurse telephoning the doctor and the doctor arriving, yet he could also see people and places as far from his home in the south of England as Scotland, several hundred miles to the north. Since he was almost certainly unconscious at the time – he believed his heart stopped beating just before the camphor injection – his account suggests that part of our consciousness can carry on independently of the body and enter a world quite unlike the one with which we are familiar.

In his out-of-body state, Geddes unwittingly became a receiver of telepathy, a subject he had no problem in taking on board:

If we accept the hypothesis that there is a psychic continuum enveloping all mankind, influenced by and influencing human brains, there is no difficulty in picturing how paranormal [sic] psychic phenomena occur. If we do not accept it they cannot be explained.

In his Edinburgh lecture he gave an account of an incident remarkably similar to some of those I have mentioned earlier, although he did not specifically say if those involved were twins:

A sister in Edinburgh has a severe heart attack as a result of shock and anxiety, because she knows intuitively that her brother, stationed in India, has met with some disaster, though no physical message of any sort has passed... This is an actual case. The knowledge, of course, was conveyed by Telepathy, but what does that mean? It is a mere word, and adds nothing to what I have just said – she felt at a distance.

Telepathy, he concluded, should be accepted as 'a primary datum of science', and in his memoirs he returned to the subject, noting that it was 'a well-attested phenomenon' for which there was abundant evidence in the animal kingdom: 'The type of intercommuncation which man thinks of as para-normal is for lowlier animals, the normal.'

KNOWING BY EXPERIENCE

Fortunately, one does not have to have a life-threatening illness in order to enter an extended or other reality of a kind that has been experienced in practically every culture from India and China to the indigenous peoples of Australia, Africa and the Americas. It has been described for centuries by mystics, saints and creative artists from Saints Paul, Augustine, Francis of Assisi, Joan of Arc and Teresa of Ávila to Dante, Bosch and Blake. One 20th-century mystic who gave a very clear account of it was George William

Russell ('AE'), who, I should add, was not only a lifelong mystic but also a down-to-earth newspaper editor with a special interest in agricultural reform. He makes himself very clear:

> *I have discovered that consciousness can exist outside the body, that we can sometimes see people who are far away from us, that we can even speak to them when they are hundreds of miles distant: I have been spoken to myself in this way. I know by experience that disembodied beings may act upon us profoundly.*[2]

Disembodied, as he made clear, did not automatically mean deceased. On one occasion he was thinking of a friend, not knowing where he was at the time, when he suddenly felt him to be near the Sphinx:

> *I did not see him in vision, but I seemed to be walking there in the night. Why did the angle of vision change as with one moving about? Did I see through his eyes? Or did I see, as in the other incident [see below], images reflected from his sphere to my own? Where does this vision end? What are its limitations?*

A good question. Later, Russell learned that his friend had indeed been spending a night by the Sphinx. The other incident he referred to was the one I mentioned briefly in Chapter 6 in which he involuntarily picked up an image of what his office colleague was thinking of at the time. He wondered if incidents like this one might explain what we call inspiration:

> *If I had written a tale and had imagined an inner room, an old mother, an absent son, a family trouble, might I not all the while be still adventuring in another's life? While we think we are imagining a character we may, so marvellous are the*

hidden ways, be really interpreting a being actually existing, brought into psychic contact with us by some affinity of sentiment or soul.

This is a very unusual case, since on two occasions Russell picked up a telepathic message in which there was no sign of crisis apart from the 'family trouble'. It may in fact be the exception that proves the rule, as I know of no other case like it.

TRAVELLING CONSCIOUSNESS

There are, however, several other examples of people who, though not particularly mystical, are able to enter another reality. One of the most successful is the New York artist and writer Ingo Swann, who has not only taken part in several controlled laboratory experiments, but was also one of those chiefly responsible for setting up the U.S. Star Gate programme in which military personnel were trained to use clairvoyance, or 'remote viewing' as they preferred to call it, for intelligence gathering.[3]

Swann began his psi career in the 1970s with a series of experiments for researchers Dr Karlis Osis and Janet Mitchell at the American Society for Psychical Research in New York. They were reviving what mesmerists of the previous century had called 'travelling clairvoyance', and although some impressive cases of this were on record, it was never very thoroughly researched. In one famous instance, the French psychologist Pierre Janet hypnotized a woman and 'sent' her to the laboratory of his colleague Charles Richet, whereupon she announced that it was on fire – as indeed it was. On another occasion she correctly reported that one of Richet's assistants had just burned himself. These promising experiments were not followed up, although Richet (a Nobel laureate in medicine) took an active interest in psychical research throughout his life.[4] Osis and Mitchell had much lost time to make up for.

Swann was a firm believer in psi when he began the

experiments, though as he put it 'I did not believe that I possessed any particular talent for it.' It soon became clear that he did, after an experiment in which he was asked to float up to the ceiling and describe what was in a specially constructed box suspended from it so that its contents could be seen only from above. After a discouragingly slow start he kept at it and was eventually able to draw accurate pictures of the objects in the box, although he was not always sure what they were. After several months of work at the ASPR, Swann produced solid evidence in support of the claims of George W. Russell and Lord Geddes (and too many others to mention here) that consciousness can indeed leave the physical body.

Swann made it all sound easy. 'Remote viewing is not much different from day dreaming,' he told an interviewer in 1978. 'You just agree with yourself that you're going to do it... and you'll start to get a flood of images.'[5]

Shortly after the New York experiments, Swann began work at Stanford Research Institute (now SRI International) in California which grew into what became known as the Star Gate programme run by the Defense Intelligence Agency. This showed for the first time ever, as far as is known, that telepathy and/or clairvoyance can be practised by just about anybody who is properly trained and supervised, and can be put to practical use. One of the best of the 30 or so military 'remote viewers', Joe McMoneagle, even won a medal for his intelligence gathering work, and the programme was given the public endorsement of President Jimmy Carter, no less, when he described how a Soviet aircraft that had crashed in Africa had been found by one of the women Star Gate viewers:

She went into a trance. And while she was in a trance, she gave some latitude and longitude figures. We focused our satellite cameras on that point, and the plane was there.[6]

Former Star Gate programme director Dr Harold Puthoff said in a

2000 interview that remote viewing had been used 'on almost every major security issue' and that there were 'file cabinets full of data that probably won't be declassified in our lifetime'.[7]

Thoughts Through Space

One earlier demonstration of remote viewing, however, was fully publicized and well witnessed at the time, and is one of the most thoroughly documented cases of its kind ever published, as well as one of the most consistently successful. There is a good deal we can still learn from it.

In 1937, a Soviet aircraft went missing on a flight over the North Pole and was assumed to have crash landed somewhere in Alaska. Its last radio message had ended 'We are going to land in...' The rest was garbled static. The Soviets were anxious to locate the plane and asked the well-known explorer Sir Hubert Wilkins to mount an air search for it. He agreed, and discussed his plans one evening with a fellow member of New York's City Club, a popular writer named Harold Sherman.

They found they shared an interest in psychic matters. Wilkins had believed in telepathy ever since his childhood in Australia and had witnessed demonstrations of it by Aborigines, while Sherman had long had psi experiences of his own. As they talked, Sherman suddenly had an idea. Wilkins had mentioned that there could be times when radio interference caused by high sunspot activity might make it impossible for him to communicate from Alaska to his New York base. Impossible, that is, by any known normal means. So, Sherman suggested, why not see if the telepathic signal could get through when the radio signal was lost?[8]

Wilkins knew perfectly well that he was going on a potentially dangerous mission. Like the Soviet pilot, he too might disappear and need rescuing. So there was a genuine need for telepathic back-up – the two men were not merely playing a parlour game.

Sherman promised to spend half an hour three times a week at 11.30 p.m. Eastern Standard Time trying to tune in to Wilkins, who in turn would keep a log of each day's events. This would eventually be compared with Sherman's notes, copies of which were to be deposited with a colleague who could verify that they were written when Sherman said they were.

Wilkins and his crew duly took off in their Lockheed Electra on 22 October, 1937. Three days later, Sherman noted in his diary:

> *I sat in my study at 380 Riverside Drive, New York City, notebook before me on desk, lights out. I awaited impressions, either in the form of mental images or strong feelings or flashes which could be translated as having a certain meaning.*

All of these began to come in at once, and over the next five months Sherman made a total of 68 entries in his notebook, recording more than 300 specific statements. He scored a bull's-eye on his first attempt, noting:

> *You in company heavy-set man or he nearby – impression, as you would say 'Wilkins signing off'.*

Wilkins had sat between two heavy-set men at dinner that evening, and had been interviewed by a Canadian radio station, the transmission ending with these exact words.

Not surprisingly, many of Sherman's impressions were of snow, ice and cold. Yet again and again he came up with an impression of something that seemed quite out of place. One evening, for instance, he wrote:

> *You in company, men in military attire, some women, evening dress, much conversation. You appear to be in evening dress yourself.*

This is not quite what one would expect an Arctic explorer to be doing, yet it was precisely what Wilkins was doing, and wearing –

the evening dress being lent to him for the occasion, an Armistice Ball in Regina, Alaska, to which he had been invited unexpectedly. A few days later Sherman picked up another smart social event which he described as 'some kind of banquet, seem to see it held in church'. He added, 'Connection school, standing in front of blackboard, chalk in hand, you give short talk.'

Right again – Wilkins had attended a banquet held in Missionary's House, Point Barrow, and that morning he had given a talk to the local schoolchildren. So it went on, Sherman correctly mentioning a fire, a toothache, a ladder, and a diamond mine, the subject of another talk that Wilkins had given on the day of Sherman's reference to it. He picked up almost the precise moment when Wilkins decided he had to give up his search for the missing Soviet plane, and named the day when the explorer would return to New York.

When they compared notes, Wilkins was impressed. 'You seem to get all the very strong thoughts and sense the vivid conditions,' he commented. In fact, very few of Sherman's statements were totally wrong, the great majority being totally right.

During the experimental period, the two men had agreed to carry out some tests using Rhine's Zener cards, Wilkins sending and Sherman receiving. The latter scored slightly above chance level, but it seems that the sender was not trying very hard at his end. 'I was not particularly interested in carrying out experiments with these cards,' Wilkins recalled, 'because it seemed to me that if there were one especially difficult way to demonstrate the possibility of thought transference, it would be with five marked cards.'

The lesson to be learned from this classic series of experiments is that telepathy works best when it has to, especially at a time of crisis or strong emotion; and when its participants are not only highly motivated to succeed but are convinced in advance that they can succeed. As I have shown, it is a lesson too many have failed to learn.

TELEPATHY SAVES A LIFE

If Wilkins had got into difficulties, he was going to try to communicate this to Sherman by concentrating on the figures for the latitude and longitude of his position, and one of three colours: red for injury, black for death of a crew member and white for all well. It is possible, to judge from Sherman's overall success rate, that in an emergency he might have been able to save lives. There is at least one case on record, in addition to that of the Powles babies I mentioned in Chapter 4, in which telepathy almost certainly did save a life. It was thoroughly investigated soon after the event, by parapsychologists J. Fraser Nicol and his wife Betty, who had worked with J. B. Rhine at Duke University, and again there is much we can learn from it.[9]

In 1955, a welder named Jack Sullivan was working alone in a deep trench in Washington Street, Boston (USA) when the sides fell in and buried him. To make matters worse he was severely burned by the red-hot pipe he had just been welding. He yelled for help but there was nobody within earshot. Then, as he recalled later, a 'vivid picture' of his workmate Tommy Whittaker had come to mind together with the thought that somehow he might be able to help him.

This seemed unlikely on the face of it because, as Jack knew, Tommy was working at another site. Yet, sure enough, he decided to stop work early so that he could pass by the Washington Street job to make sure all was well. He seems to have had no clear idea that Jack was in danger, just a nagging feeling that he should go there, though as he left he did remark to a workmate, 'There might be something wrong.'

He reached the site just in time. The first thing he noticed was that Jack's generator was still running, and it was not like him to make a careless mistake like that – forgetting to turn it off when he had gone home. Then he noticed that the cable disappeared underground, and at about that moment Jack managed to get a hand above ground, and Tommy was able to rescue him. As Jack was badly burned, it is quite possible he would not have had the strength to dig himself out, and that nobody would have found him until the following day.

One researcher who learned a great deal from this case was the maverick freelance scientist and author Andrija Puharich who was, to put it mildly, controversial.[x] He is best known as the man who brought Uri Geller to the USA, and who went to Brazil to study the 'rusty knife' surgeon known as Arigó. He also became involved in magic mushrooms, and alienated most of the scientific community by claiming to be in touch with extraterrestrials. To many, he was the archetypal mad scientist, though to me, who met him several times and had long conversations with him, he was one of the most interesting and charming people I have ever met.

In his early days he did some excellent research into telepathy in his own laboratory, using well-known star performers such as Eileen Garrett and Peter Hurkos as subjects, not only piling up successful results but also developing and testing his theory, which he published in 1962, of how telepathy actually worked. This is something surprisingly few have attempted to do until recently.

ADRENERGIA AND CHOLINERGIA

He began with the observation that, as all the evidence showed, for telepathy to take place both the sender and the receiver had to be in very specific and very different states of mind at the time. He called these states adrenergia and cholinergia, the first being the state in which our sympathetic nervous systems are dominant, and the latter one in which the other nervous system, the parasympathetic, takes charge. These two states form the autonomic nervous system, which looks after things normally beyond our conscious control, such as heart-beat, blood flow and digestion. However, the two states are very different.

In the adrenergic state the heart beat speeds up, the blood vessels contract, and the pupils of the eyes dilate as we work ourselves up to a state of readiness for action. Our kidneys secrete a substance called epinephrine, also known as adrenalin because it originates in the adrenal glands. When we get the adrenalin flowing, as we say, we are in a state of excitement, effort, crisis, panic, danger or imminent death.

If adrenergia is the upper, cholinergia is the downer. It is activated by the compound acetylcholine, which leads via the parasympathetic nervous system to slowing the heart beat, lowering blood pressure, constricting the pupils, making the digestion run smoothly and generally calming us down.

Where telepathy is concerned, the sender has to be in an adrenergic state, which need not be as extreme as those facing sudden death are in. The sender does not have to be in a panic, but has at the very least to be *intending* to send. The receiver, on the other hand, should be in as cholinergic a state as possible – relaxed, hypnotized or mesmerized, daydreaming, asleep or doing nothing in particular; or, for laboratory experiments, simply intending to receive.

Studying the Boston case, Puharich saw at once that Sullivan must have suffered a 'massive adrenergia' when the trench caved in on him, whereas Whittaker was in an ideal state of cholinergia at the time. True, he was not asleep or even resting, in fact he was also welding, as Jack had been. This, he told the Nicols, was a state in which 'all sorts of irrelevant things run through your mind, and you hardly know you are working'. Routine physical work, in Puharich's view, could be perfect for telepathic reception especially if the work is repetitive and does not need to be thought about. Heat would also help, whether from the sun or from a welding torch.

Always one to boldly go where other psi researchers feared to tread, Puharich (who was a qualified doctor) thought up some ingenious ways of inducing the two ideal states in his laboratory. Cholinergia was no problem – he simply gave his subject a dose of the 'sacred' mushroom *Amanita muscaria*, with dramatic effect. In a picture-matching test (a forerunner of the Ganzfeld method I described in Chapter 6), one subject scored 10 out of 10 in a few seconds despite the fact that he seemed to be more than somewhat intoxicated. The probability of this being due to chance was one in a million. (In most kinds of scientific experiment, a chance probability of a mere one in twenty is regarded as significant.)

Puharich repeated this experiment with four sceptical reporters as subjects, using numbers instead of pictures as targets. Before they took their sacred mouthfuls they scored almost exactly at chance level, but after 45 minutes the probability rate shot up to one in 200, which is very highly significant. A couple of hours later the effects of the mushroom had worn off and the scores were back to chance level. (Note to readers: do NOT take funny mushrooms except under expert and professional supervision. I have seen what they can do and it is not a pretty sight.)

Inducing adrenergia was not so easy, since you cannot put laboratory subjects into real crisis conditions, at least not if you want them to come back for more testing, but Puharich had a stroke of luck. One of his regular subjects, Peter Hurkos (who later became famous for his psychic detective work) had an extreme fear of electricity, so Puharich had him sit on a metal plate containing 20,000 volts of direct current. He knew this was quite harmless but Hurkos was not so sure. 'I could see grave doubts and fears written all over his face as the experiment began,' Puharich noted.

Even he was surprised by the results. With Hurkos, in his artificially induced state of adrenergia, acting as sender in a standard matching test, the receiver made more than twice as many correct guesses as when Hurkos was in his normal state. Puharich repeated this experiment seven times and reckoned he had proved his point.

MENTAL GRAVITY?

I have been using the words sender and receiver for convenience but, as Puharich was probably the first to point out, the words may be misleading. He saw the process of telepathic transfer not as a centrifugal one, like the broadcasting of radio waves, but as a state of concentration in which the force was just the opposite – centripetal. He explained:

> *The sender does not send anything out, but rather serves as a centre of attraction drawing to him the attention of the receiver. It is as though the sender creates a mental vacuum toward which the receiver's mind is drawn. The sender by his need and desire prepares a mental stage; the receiver in turn populates the stage with his own symbols and images.*

So while telepathy may look as if it were operating like a kind of mental radio, in fact it may be more like mental gravity. Both of these can operate over enormous distances, yet there is an obvious difference between them: telepathy is selective and gravity is not. With very few possible exceptions, the message gets from A to B and not to C, D or the rest of the world. Jack Sullivan's distress signal was picked up by one of the few people he knew who was likely to be able to save him, and who luckily happened to be in a suitably cholinergic state. If he had left work and gone to a noisy bar for a beer with his mates he might not have got the message at all.

As I hope I have made clear, many people do not get such messages. Even the majority of identical twins do not seem to get them. Why would this be? One theory is that telepathy today is no more than a faint echo of what it was when it was needed for survival, as it still is by many animals, and appears only at moments of crisis or, as it were, by mistake, as in this example from an unexpected source:

> *They say that twins have psychic powers which enable one to know what the other is thinking, even from a great distance, and I have found this to be true over the years. Ron and I pick up on each other's moods. One time we sent each other letters which crossed in the post. We each revealed to the other that we were going to buy a budgie and a cage.*[11]

It may seem surprising that Britain's most notorious twins, gangsters Ronald and Reginald Kray, should have wanted pet birds, and even more surprising that they felt they had to write to tell each other so. There was no survival at stake here, and it may well be that some cases of telepathy are no more than accidental.

All the same, by far the best evidence for it comes from three sources: identical twins, mothers and babies, and pets, especially dogs, and their owners. I have concentrated on twins in this book because, as I have said, nobody seems to have done so before, whereas two researchers have done useful work in connection with the other groups. More about them in a moment, but first I want to discuss a little-known experiment which, though rather unpleasant, taught us a good deal about telepathy. It did not involve pets or people, but mice in a Siberian laboratory.

There, a scientist named Sergei V. Speransky (a former student of the leading Soviet parapsychologist Leonid Vasiliev) set out to study the effects of a certain poison on living systems, so he took four groups of identical male mice, put them in separate cages side by side, and gave them all the same food. Then there was a delay. It seems the poison got lost in the post, so Speransky decided to do an experiment of his own.[12]

Since the mice had lived together for some time, he reckoned they would be bonded together much as a human family would be. He wondered what would happen if he divided a group of them into two subgroups, leaving one on the ground floor, taking the other up to the fourth floor and subjecting one of the subgroups only to what he called 'purposeful influence'.

He duly fed all the mice as usual for a control period, then began to starve the upstairs lot for five hours at a time, to see if the downstairs ones would pick up the hunger signal and eat more to make up for their distant colleagues' starvation. The experiment was run 30 times, fortunately without starving any of the mice to death, and on 27 occasions the normally-fed mice did eat more than when the upstairs group were brought down in between starvation periods and fed normally.

I have been assured by a scientist who visited Speransky's laboratory in the Soviet high-tech capital Novosibirsk that the experiments were genuine, but they worked only if they were run for one day only, letting the mice settle down to normal life before trying it again. 'You need to surprise them,' he said.[13] Here, it seems, we see telepathy at its most subtle, operating at a completely unconscious level.

THE DOG AT THE WINDOW

Fortunately, there are ways in which animals can take part in experiments in which they are not mistreated, and in fact do not have to do anything they would not do anyway. The best of these so far have involved dogs, and it may be that the dog–owner bond is just as strong as that between a mother and her child or between identical twins, perhaps even stronger. Children grow up and leave home, most twins develop a degree of independence, yet the dog–owner bond is for life as far as the dog is concerned. So it is not surprising that this is where we find some very good evidence for telepathy.

Some of the best has been collected by biologist and author Rupert Sheldrake, from a wide variety of sources in several countries.[14] He has found that dogs seem to be the most telepathic, followed by cats, horses and parrots, 'with humans trailing far behind'. Dogs, he has found, know when their owners are coming home, they howl when their owners die, however far away they may be, they even react to a ringing telephone when their owners are on the line but not when anybody else is. They can get all excited about going for a walk when their owner merely *thinks* 'walkies'. They can respond to a high-frequency whistle before owners actually blow it. Most remarkably of all they can find their way home after being lost hundreds, even allegedly thousands of miles away.

Cats, it seems, have a speciality of their own: going missing on the day they are supposed to go to the vet. Sheldrake contacted all 65 veterinary clinics in his local phone book and asked if they had any experience of appointments having to be cancelled because the cat could not be found. All except one said yes they had, quite frequently. The other one said no, because they no longer made appointments – 'people simply had to turn up with their cat'.

Cats do not make very cooperative experimental subjects, but dogs do. With the help of dog owner Pamela Smart, Sheldrake has carried out a long series of experiments with her male mongrel terrier Jaytee. Their observations of his behaviour began in 1991, when he was about two years old, and were still continuing a decade later. Pamela used to have a regular job, and would leave the dog with her parents in their ground-floor flat in which there is a full-length picture window. Mr and Mrs Smart soon got used to seeing Jaytee get up and go to the window at about the time Pamela set off for home, and since she always came back at about the same time they just assumed the dog had a good sense of time and nothing more.

Then, in 1993, Pamela was made redundant and no longer had a regular daily schedule. She could go out for a few minutes or several hours, often not knowing herself when she would start to head for home. Her parents would not know either, but it seemed that Jaytee invariably did. Whenever Pamela came home, there he was at the window, where he had been for about the same time her journey home had taken.

Sheldrake became involved in 1994 after Pamela Smart had responded to his appeal for volunteers. At his suggestion, she kept a log of the exact times she went out, how far she went, and when she decided it was time to go home. Her parents also made notes about the dog's movements to the window during his owner's absence.

Over a nine-month period, the Smarts kept such a record of 100 homecomings, and found that Jaytee was at the window for 85 of them. They found normal explanations for all but three of his failures – such as feeling sick, being distracted by passing cats or the bitch on heat upstairs, or being left alone with Mr Smart, of whom he was rather afraid.

A team from Austrian State TV filmed one of these experiments, using two cameras, one aimed at Jaytee and the other recording the moment when Pamela was told by one of the TV team that it was time to start for home. This was nearly four hours after she had gone out. As can be seen on the split-screen film, Jaytee's ears pricked up at almost the exact moment that Pamela was given her orders. Eleven seconds later he walked slowly to the window, sat down, ears still up, and just waited.

The Austrian footage was subjected to some highly tendentious criticism in a Channel 4 programme misleadingly entitled *Secrets of the Psychics*, in which extreme sceptic Dr Richard Wiseman showed a clip from one of four experiments he had carried out with Jaytee, who was seen walking to the window several times. Wiseman alleged that the dog 'was visiting the window about once every 10 minutes so under those conditions it is not surprising he was there when his owner was thinking of returning home'.

What was surprising was to find that the time code visible on the clip suggested that two of Jaytee's trips to the window were in fact the same trip shown twice. It is hard to imagine a professional editor doing this by mistake, and if it was deliberate data massaging it was an example of the kind of fakery the programme was purporting to unmask.[15]

COLLECTIVE THINKING

Studies of collective animal behaviour provide especially persuasive evidence for telepathy. One only has to watch a flock of birds flying in rather loose formation with different birds out in front from time to time to ask, as the naturalist Edmond Selous did in 1931: 'how, without some process of thought transference so rapid as to amount practically to simultaneous collective thinking, are these things to be explained?' How, indeed?

More recent studies of slowed-down bird flight films have shown that although some birds do turn first, they can be anywhere in the flock and cause what Sheldrake describes as 'a wave radiating from the site of initiation' as the other birds turn an average of 15 thousandths of a second after their neighbours. This is considerably less than tests with captive birds have shown to be their minimum reaction time to an unexpected stimulus. This seems particularly good evidence for a group mind at work – there may in fact be no need for a radiating wave or single 'site of initiation', just a mind.

Fish, ants, termites, bees, wasps, wolves, elks, caribou and several other living beings can also be seen to display what looks like a group mind, and it is surely no coincidence that many of the kinds of information that seem to be communicated telepathically by them, which Sheldrake lists as 'fear, alarm, excitement, calls for help, calls to go to a particular place, anticipation of arrivals or departures, and distress or dying' are the same as those communicated by people?

I CAN READ YOUR MIND

The last of the three groups at the top of the telepathy-proneness scale, that of parents and children, has been meticulously documented by American clinical psychiatrist Dr Berthold Eric Schwarz.[16] He took the trouble to record a total of 1,520 episodes involving himself, his wife Ardis and their two children Eric and Lisa, starting in 1958 when Lisa was 20 months old and ending in 1970 when she was 14 and Eric was 12.

Lisa began to say surprising things well before her second birthday. One day, as her father was reading a book, he thought of phoning a friend to invite him to dinner, but hesitated, asking himself if he wouldn't rather stay at home and read? At that moment Lisa exclaimed 'Telephone!'

Eric also got off to an early start. Just before he was two, Ardis was making his bed and feeling that he should spend more time looking at picture books, thinking of one book in particular and wondering where it was, but saying nothing, whereupon Eric went out of the room and came back holding it. On another occasion, Schwarz was looking in vain for a special red pen in his office and getting rather annoyed, when Eric ran downstairs and greeted him with the words 'Here, Daddy, is the red pen.'

Reading an article about financier J. P. Morgan's last words: 'I must go up the hill', Schwarz was wondering what they meant when Lisa suddenly announced 'Up the hill! Up the hill!' When she was six, she was going for a walk with her father when he remembered he needed to blow up her new balloon. 'Daddy, will you blow up my balloon?' she asked at once, and when he looked startled she added, 'Ha ha, I can read your mind!'

These examples (and there were over 1,500 more) were generally of fairly trivial incidents, although Schwarz noted that many served real needs such as the discovery of missing objects or prompting a child to do something their parents silently wanted them to do. In addition to these, Schwarz also mentions 'countless' instances of telepathy between him and his wife, and also noted that over a 10-year period in which he gave psychotherapy to 2,013 patients, he recorded 'one or more presumed telepathic events' on 1,443 occasions. That is a lot of telepathic events. Do we really need any more evidence? I think not, but cannot resist mentioning one of one of Schwarz's most striking cases.

It took place on 22 November, 1963, a day most of those then alive remember very well. Ardis was on the phone when Eric, then aged five, suddenly rushed into the room and turned the radio on full blast. He had never done this before.

Schwarz yelled at him to turn it off, but he didn't. This was also unusual as he tended to do what he was told. Ardis then hung up and the phone rang again at once. It was Schwarz's mother calling to tell him to switch on the radio immediately – President Kennedy had just been shot.

CHAPTER 10

QUANTUM TWINS

21ST-CENTURY PHYSICS

One of the following statements must be true:

1. Every incident described in this book – every single one of them – has a normal explanation. Most of them seem to be beyond scientific explanation, so it is more likely that they are all due to chance coincidence or misreporting.
2. Even if only a few of the incidents are true, and I have no reason to suggest that any of them are not, they are still generally considered inexplicable in terms of science as presently understood. Therefore science, especially physics, is incomplete.

It is easy to dismiss the first statement on purely statistical grounds. The chances that so many people would independently invent or misreport exactly the same incidents are too remote to be worth considering. So we are left with the second. I was delighted to find, when I attended the annual conference of the Society for Psychical Research in September 2001, that at least some scientists are well aware that science is incomplete. One of these was Nobel laureate Professor Brian Josephson, the physicist who got into all that trouble for daring to suggest that telepathy might be explained by quantum theory. During a talk that I will not attempt to summarize, he specifically stated, 'We need a new physics,' and although he did add 'and it's not too clear what it is,' he predicted that 'the new physics will put the mind properly into science.'

Professor Bernard Carr, a well-known astrophysicist who was also the president of the SPR, was equally forthright. He reminded us that our view of reality has regularly been turned upside down over the centuries – Newtonian physics had to take atomic physics on board, and was then superseded by Einstein's special and general relativity theories. Then along came quantum theory, now widely held to be the greatest advance in science of the 20th century even though nobody seems to understand it, and now in a new century it was time for a new paradigm, or model of reality, one that would have to include the kind of experiences I have been describing in this book.

I left the conference with my head reeling from so much talk (from professors of physics) of particle-wave dualities, wormholes in space, 10-dimensional superstrings and much else besides including 'quantum spookiness' of which more below. Yet I was encouraged to have been told that while telepathy may have been impossible in terms of 20th-century science, it was becoming increasingly possible in that of the 21st century. I also felt I had caught a glimpse of an explanation for telepathy, and an explanation for why twin telepathy is special. You are reading it here first, and I will try to keep it simple.

THE EMPATHY FIELD

In Chapter 3 I described how Drs Duane and Behrendt claimed back in 1965 to have observed 'extrasensory induction' with pairs of twins, but despite limited support from Dr Esser and his plethysmograph experiments, were either furiously attacked or just ignored. It now seems they may have been right all the time .

When any two people are emotionally close to each other, whether they are twins or not, they become part of what we can call an empathy field. This can vary in strength according to the closeness of those concerned, and as I pointed out in the previous chapter, the three closest bonds are those of identical twins, mothers and babies, and dogs and their owners. These will therefore have the strongest empathy fields.

Others will also have such fields, though not so strong. These include non-identical twins, brothers and sisters, couples married or otherwise, good friends and work colleagues. Temporary fields can also be created to order, as in the case of laboratory experimenters and their subjects.

In conventional physics, a field is simply a region of space in which there are physical properties that can be determined at any part of it. The most familiar one is the magnetic field made visible by iron filings on a piece of card with a magnet underneath it. There are also electromagnetic and gravitational fields, which are fairly well understood and put to practical use even if we have not yet worked out what Newton called the 'tractions' of gravity. Fields can be small- or large-scale, and some are enormous – the magnetosphere which contains the earth's magnetic field, for instance, stretches for some 40,000 miles on the day side of the planet and nearly a million miles on the night side. There is no problem, then, in imagining a field that can cover the whole world.

I seem to hear a distant cry of 'What on earth do you mean by an empathy field? Where's the evidence for it?' Fair question. Here is the answer ...

THE INFORMATIONAL MATRIX

In 1994 a team headed by Mexican psychologist Jacobo Grinberg-Zylberbaum of the National Autonomous University in Mexico City published the results of at least 50 experiments carried out over a period of 18 years which, they reckoned, indicated the existence of a 'hyperfield'.[1] This is precisely what my proposed empathy field would have to be – the prefix 'hyper' implying that it is larger than we would have thought possible.

The experimental set-up was very simple. The researchers looked for pairs of volunteers who were emotionally close, whether related or not, and who were regular meditators. These were asked to sit together inside a Faraday cage, a room designed to make any normal communication with anybody inside impossible, and just meditate together for 20 minutes, doing their best to achieve a state of 'empathic non-verbal communication'. At the same time, they were wired to a brainwave recorder (EEG), and chart recordings showed that some of the pairs could display virtually identical patterns, which control groups of total strangers could not. Some were better at it than others, and it seemed to depend on the intensity of their relationship.

This was interesting in itself, but it was hardly proof of telepathy. Yet there was more to come. After the 20-minute meditation period, one member of each pair stayed put while the other was taken to another Faraday cage several metres away and wired to another EEG. Both were asked to stay in their empathy mode and go on thinking of each other.

Then, without warning, a randomly controlled device gave one of the pair a series of stimuli including noises, flashes of light and 'short, intense but not painful electric shocks'. These produced the expected blips on the chart of the subject who was being stimulated – and sometimes, though not always, they also produced identical blips on the chart of the distant one who was not being stimulated at all and had no idea what was going on in the other cage. It worked in only 25 per cent of the pairs, but when it did work it seemed to have proved that communication can be seen to take place under conditions in which normal communication is impossible. It was clear evidence for telepathy at work.

Grinberg-Zylberbaum found that those who did demonstrate this could invariably do it again, but those who could not were unable to do it on subsequent sessions. It was something some pairs could do all the time and others could not do any of the time. The researcher reckoned it must have something to do with 'the intensity of the empathic relationship achieved', since the best results came from 'a young couple who were deeply in love', showing 'an extraordinary morphological similarity in their EEGs'.

He did not use the word telepathy, preferring to speak in terms of 'a pre-space structure that forms a kind of informational matrix', a concept based on the ideas of physicist David Bohm, who put forward a lengthy case (something else I will not attempt to summarize) for the existence of another level of reality beyond our familiar one.[2]

Now that we have good evidence for the existence of an empathy field, the problem of how the spontaneous telepathic message gets from A to B no longer arises; it does not have to go to B because it is already there (and everywhere else in the field). B simply becomes aware of it because of what looks like resonance of a kind that operates only when A and B are in the right states of mind – adrenergic for A and cholinergic for B, in Puharich's terms.

The subjects in the Mexican experiments were both in the same state of mind – or should that be in states of the same mind? – yet the stimuli must have induced brief moments of adrenergia that were transmitted automatically and picked up in the other half of the empathy field. The researchers were planning long-distance experiments with subjects thousands of miles apart, but these do not appear to have been done, and I gather that Dr Grinberg-Zylberbaum has either retired or died. However, no experiment could be easier to repeat.

QUANTUM SPOOKINESS

Now for the 'quantum spookiness'. This is not the place for an explanation of quantum theory, and this is not the author to attempt it. There are several excellent popular books on it (see bibliography) and if I admit I do not understand it, I am in good company: 'I think I can safely say that nobody understands quantum mechanics', as physicist Richard Feynman famously declared shortly after getting his Nobel Prize for his work on it.

So as promised I will keep it simple. The quantum was born on 14 December 1900, when Max Planck introduced the idea of energy as something that came not in a continuous stream but in tiny and discrete units which he called quanta. This may not sound very exciting in itself, but it eventually led to Niels Bohr's

Quantum Theory of 1927 and on to a physical world that Newton would have found as incomprehensible as many of us still do. It is a world in which, at least at microscopic level, solid matter has disappeared altogether in a cloud of hidden variables, superposition of states, and something known rather confusingly as non-locality.

This is where it gets spooky. Non-locality was one of the key predictions of quantum theory, and without worrying for the time being what it actually means, let us look at some of its implications, as neatly summarized by physicist J. P. McEvoy:

1. The interaction does not diminish with distance.
2. It can act instantaneously [i.e. faster than the speed of light].
3. It links up locations without crossing space.[3]

He adds, rather tentatively, that the only popular instances of such non-locality he could think of were the interactions of voodoo and 'perhaps extra-sensory perception'. He might have added the interactions observed and recorded by Grynberg-Zylberbaum, who commented that 'the interaction between brains seems to behave similarly to the interaction observed between elementary particles in the experiments of Aspect.' Alain Aspect was the French scientist who showed in 1982 that once a pair of photons had been emitted simultaneously from an atom and were thus 'entangled' in quantum jargon, they remained entangled even when separated and fired off in opposite directions.[4] Moreover, it seemed that one would react to what was being done to the other. His photons were only a few metres apart in his laboratory, but in 1997 Swiss researchers repeated this experiment over a distance of several miles.[5]

All this was done in order to disprove a thought-experiment known as the Einstein-Podolsky-Rosen paradox,[6] which was intended to show that what Einstein called 'spooky action at a distance' was impossible, because it would involve speeds faster than that of light – the ultimate taboo. An article on the Swiss work in the leading journal *Science* was headlined 'Quantum Spookiness Wins, Einstein Loses in Photon Test'.

John Gribbin, one of the authors I referred to above, emphasises that 'Non-local behaviour has been proved to occur by real experiments.'[7] It is, he adds, 'as if the two quantum entities… remain tangled up with one another for ever, so that when one is prodded the other twitches, instantaneously, no matter how far apart they are.' The coin, I hope, is beginning to drop.

Another scientist-author, Danah Zohar, gets straight to the point I am about to make: 'The gist of the EPR paradox,' she wrote in 1990, 'can be understood by imagining the fate of a hypothetical set of identical twins.'[8] She goes on to describe a thought-experiment in which a twin in London is kicked downstairs and breaks a leg. 'No one would argue that any shared genetic material could explain it if the twin living in California were then to suffer a similar fall.' Yet, she adds, if quantum theory is correct and Einstein was wrong (as is now generally agreed):

In fact, when the London twin is kicked, the California twin will suffer an identical fall at exactly the same moment and break his leg too, although no one has kicked him.

She adds in a footnote that the idea of using twins as an example was hers and not Einstein's, and the same example has been used by several others, none of whom seems aware that imaginary experiments such as the one mentioned above describe exactly what does happen to identical twins. (Sir Roger Penrose, one of Britain's leading theoretical physicists, has suggested that consciousness is an effect of quantum entanglement, and in a reply to a questioner at a lecture he gave in 2001 he admitted that this might have implications for the twin bond.)[9]

Twins have reacted, often quite dramatically, when the other one is falling downstairs, breaking a leg or a nose, having a painful injection several miles away, getting stuck in railings or a car seat belt, burning a hand, suffocating, giving birth, strangling his wife or being shot dead. They have shown beyond any reasonable doubt that there is a form of communication across space that cannot possibly be explained in terms of pre-quantum science.

However, before anyone nominates me for a Nobel Prize for solving the mystery of telepathy, I should add that it cannot yet be explained in terms of post-quantum science either. Several of my scientist friends have said more or less the same thing: quantum theory applies to events only at submicroscopic levels and there is no evidence to suggest that it can be applied to macroscopic objects such as people.

AN ENTANGLED SYSTEM

Point taken, yet the analogy remains strong. Identical twins have been a correlated or 'entangled' system ever since they split apart in the womb, being literally entangled until birth. Even after birth they have remained closely bonded, sometimes all their lives, their bond being one of the strongest there is. So it is not surprising that if telepathy exists, they will experience it in a particularly intense way, picking up the signal at full strength. This is something that non-twins generally do not do although there are occasional exceptions, as I have already pointed out. This is why, as I have suggested, the proper study of telepathy is identical twins.

One of the best ways to study them, I suggest, is along the lines of the work done in Mexico even though this did not involve twins. The team, one of whose members was quantum theorist Amit Goswami, make their conclusions very clear:

The human brain is capable of establishing close relationships with other brains when it interacts with them appropriately, and may sustain such an interaction even at a distance.[10]

They specifically refer to their experimental couples as 'a correlated system whose parts, separated individual brains before interaction, become one system after interaction', and they insist that there could be 'no room for doubt about the existence of an unusual phenomenon'. I suspect that if they had used identical twins, and very young ones as in the Spanish experiments I described in Chapter 4, they would have been even more successful.

In a book published in 2001 with the provocative title *Physics of the Soul*, Goswami made his views even more explicit. A former professor of Theoretical Science at the University of Oregon with more than 30 years' experience of teaching physics, he now insists that the fundamental stuff of the universe is not matter but 'a nonlocal domain of consciousness that transcends space and time'. This being so, it is only to be expected that if two people are suitably 'correlated'(i.e. bonded or entangled) they will pick up each other's sensations at a distance – any distance – although they may not always be consciously aware that they are doing so. 'Does this sound preposterous?' Goswami asks, and replies:

In truth, such nonlocal mutual influence and communication between humans has been known for millennia in the domain of mental thought. It's called telepathy.[11]

So there. For telepathy to happen, though, there seem to be three requirements:

1. A bond, permanent or temporary, between sender and receiver; the closer the bond the stronger the signal.
2. Sender and receiver must be in appropriate states of mind, the former 'adrenalized', the word Aily Biggs used to describe how she felt at the time of her frightening experience on that misty Scottish hillside, and the receiver in a much calmer state; and
3. The sender must be faced with a fairly powerful stimulus.

These rules apply, of course, only to cases in which a message is sent. There may be another kind of telepathy which operates only at the unconscious level, leading to such apparent coincidences as buying the same presents or writing identical exam papers. This is naturally very hard to investigate and is easily confused with coincidences of purely genetic origin.

You do not have to be a twin, a parent or a dog to experience telepathy, although it seems to help. We can imagine a sort of Richter scale in which some identical twins (but not all), pets and owners, and parents and small children can register nine or ten (or more – the original Richter scale has no upper limit); while others register at a much lower level and others never register at all.

It should be clear by now that the best evidence we have for telepathy comes from identical twins of a certain personality type, as identified by the Toronto team. They alone, with rare exceptions, get not only the message but also the physical sensation, the bruise or the blister, and even – as in the Henderson case – the apparition.

I also have mentioned several cases in which those involved were not related or emotionally entangled yet still shared a common bond. Jack Sullivan and Tommy Whittaker were workmates, Harold Sherman and Sir Hubert Wilkins were fellow club members both of whom happened to be exceptionally psi-prone, while Carl Sargent and I had common interests as members of the Society for Psychical Research, although at the time of our Ganzfeld session I did not know him very well and ours was a short-term entanglement. If he had fallen down a hole or got lost in Alaska the following week I doubt if I would have been able to help. Likewise, when twins are separated at birth and adopted, their bond breaks up, although their genetic similarity obviously remains and will lead to any number of similarities found when they are reunited. This need have nothing to do with telepathy although they, and others, may think otherwise.

One day, I hope, some new Einstein will come up with an equation, like e=mc^2 , in which 'e' stands for degree of bonding or entanglement, 'm' for strength of stimulus and 'c' for the state of mind of the receiver. It may not be as neat as this, but I hope this suggestion, from somebody with no scientific qualifications whatever, will prompt would-be Einsteins to start thinking about something they may not have thought much about before and come up with special and general theories of telepathy. This not only happens, as Upton Sinclair insisted, on the basis of evidence that was good enough to impress Einstein and has never been seriously challenged. It also matters for a simple reason that nobody has yet spelled out more clearly than Sinclair did in 1930:

There is new knowledge here, close to the threshold, waiting for us; and we should not let ourselves be repelled by the seeming triviality of the phenomena, for it is well known that some of the greatest discoveries have come from the following up of just such trivial clues.[12]

Seventy years later, you could say that again.

NOTES AND REFERENCES

All cases not listed in these notes were collected by the author.

Chapter 1
1 *The Times*, 28 November 1975, p.1.
2 McWhirter (1976) p.2.
3 *Cutting Edge*, Channel 4, 3 February 1997.
4 Watson (1984), p.200.
5 Segal (n.d.).
6 Shields (1962), p.94.
7 Agrippa, Paracelsus: cited in Inglis (1992), pp.97–8.
8 Bell (1964).

Chapter 2
1 Dumas (1988), pp.28, 141.
2 Dixon (1824), p.43.
3 Baume (1863).
4 Galton (1876): cited in Galton (1883), p.165.
5 Vanderbilt and Furness (1959), p.xi.
6 cited in Oppenheim (1985), pp.355–71.
7 Gurney, Myers and Podmore (1886), vol. 1, pp.279–83, vol 2, pp.46–7.
8 Newman (1942), pp.20–4.
9 Scheinfeld (1967), pp.226–7.
10 *Journal of Parapsychology*: Kubis and Rouke (1937), Stuart (1946), Rogers (1960).
11 Rosambeau (1987), p.142.
12 Lorimer (1999), p.19.
13 cited in Koestler (1986), p.247.

Chapter 3
1 Sommer *et al* (1961).
2 Duane and Behrendt (1965).
3 Tart *et al.* in Corliss (1982), pp.300–5.
4 Wright (1997), pp.52–3.
5 Ostrander and Schroeder(1971), p.291.

6 Esser *et al* (1967).
7 Barron and Mordkoff (1968).
8 Schmeidler (1943).
9 Medhurst (1968).
10 Ullman *et al* (1989), pp.87–8.
11 France and Hogan (1973); Nash and Buzby (1965).
12 Blackmore and Chamberlain (1993).
13 Charlesworth (1975).
14 Robichon (1989).

Chapter 4
1 Gavilán Fontanet (1976); Zorab (1978).
2 Spinelli (1983).
3 cited in Williams (1982).
4 Wright (1997), p.52, and personal communication (2000).
5 Radio programme: LBC *Night Line*, 28 September 1981.
6 cited in Gaddis and Gaddis (1972), pp.99–100.
7 Greensmiths: *Beyond Belief*, BBC Radio 4, 26 August 1980.
8 *Memories are Made of This*, BBC Radio 4, 5 June 2001.
9 Campbell (1995).
10 Rosambeau (1987), p.152.

Chapter 5
1 Jung (1955), Koestler (1972), Inglis (1990)
2 Jung (1955), pp.142–3.
3 Jung (1963), p.152.
4 Begley *et al* (1987).
5 *Esther*, BBC 2, 12 February 1997; *Mysteries with Carol Vorderman*, BBC 2, 2 December 1997.
6 Lambe, Hust, Crominski, Youngblood: Sieveking (1981).
7 Vanderbilt and Furness (1959), pp.xi–xii
8 Watson (1984), pp.101–40.
9 *The Times*, 5 August 1988, p.2.
10 *The Times*, 4 June 1994, p.2.
11 *Fortean Times*, January 2000, p.10.

12 *San Jose Mercury News*, 7 March 2002.
13 Allen (1965) pp.78–82.
14 Gǎrdescu (1993).

Chapter 6
1 Puységur (1809), p.49.
2 Townshend (1844), p.343.
3 Escudero: in *Mysteries with Carol Vorderman*, BBC 2, 10 November 1998. Kashpirovsky: Vinogradova (1998).
4 Crowe (1848), pp.11–12.
5 Prudence Bernard: Dingwall (1967), pp.145–57.
6 Oppenheim (1985), pp.25–6.
7 Warcollier (1938).
8 Sinclair (1930).
9 Radin (1997), pp.78–85, 129.

Chapter 7
1 Carrington (1919), pp.198–9.
2 Montgomery (1982), p.231.
3 Cooper (1997), p.180.
4 Gummer (1963), pp.20, 27, 64–5.
5 I.Wilder (1985) p.xiii.
6 McWhirter (1976), p.5.
7 Rosambeau (1987) pp.142–54.
8 Personal communication (2000).
9 Bohm (1984).

Chapter 8
1 *News of the World*, 30 January 2000, p.27.
2 Conway (1988) and cited in Milton (1994), pp.123–9.
3 Winston: *The Secret Life of Twins*, BBC 1, 21 July 1999.
4 *Esther* (BBC2, 12 February 1997); *Kilroy* (BBC 1, 19 April and 23 July 1999); *The Oprah Winfrey Show* (Channel 5, 16 June 1998); *Vanessa*, (BBC1, 24 June 1999).
5 *The Paranormal World of Paul McKenna*, Carlton TV, 24 June 1997.
6 *Sunday Mirror*, 8 February 2000, p.26.

7 *Counterblast: Where Scientists Fear to Tread*, BBC 2, 23 April 1998.
8 Milton (1994), pp.84, 85.
9 Josephson (2001); the *Observer*, 30 September 2001, p.10; the *Daily Mail*, 1 October 2001, p.11; *Today*, BBC Radio 4, 1 October 2001.
10 Newton: *Optics*, 2nd ed., 1718.

Chapter 9
1 Geddes (1937), Geddes (1952), pp.350–4.
2 Russell (AE) (1918), pp.xi, 50–1.
3 Mitchell (1985), pp.1–10.
4 Inglis (1992), pp.345–6.
5 Rogo (1988), p.198.
6 cited in Schnabel (1997), p.215.
7 in *Natural Mystery – ESP*. Channel 5, 24 July 2000.
8 Wilkins and Sherman (1971), pp.120, 245, 293, 308, 335, 425–39.
9 Nicol and Nicol (1957), (1958).
10 Puharich (1973), pp.15–22.
11 Kray (1991), p.140.
12 Speransky (1981).
13 Z. Rejdák, personal communication, 1983.
14 Sheldrake (1999).
15 Schwarz (1971).

Chapter 10
1 Grinberg-Zylberbaum (1994); Grinberg-Zylberbaum *et al* (1994).
2 Bohm (1980).
3 McEvoy and Zarate (1996), pp.170, 173.
4 Aspect *et al* (1982).
5 Watson (1997).
6 Einstein *et al.* (1935).
7 Gribbin (1995), p.24.
8 Zohar (1990), pp.19–20.
9 cited in Matthews (2001).
10 Grinberg-Zylberbaum *et al* (1994).
11 Goswani (2001), pp.34–5
12 Sinclair (1971), pp.161–2.

BIBLIOGRAPHY

Allen, T. (1965), 'The Twins Who Willed Their Death' in C.Fuller, (ed.), *Strange Fate*, New York: Paperback Library, 1965.

Aspect, A., Dalibard, J. and Roger, G. (1982), 'Experimental test of Bell's inequalities using time-varying analyzers', *Physical Review Letters* 49(25), 1804–7.

Barron, F. and Mordkoff, A. M. (1968), 'An attempt to relate creativity to possible extrasensory empathy as monitored by physiological arousal in identical twins', *Journal of the American Society for Psychical Research* 62 (1), 73–9.

Baume, Dr (1863) 'Singulier cas de folie suicide chez deux frères jumeaux – Coïncidences bizarres', *Annales Médico-Psychologiques*, 4 série, vol. 1, 312–3.

Begley, S. et al. (1987), 'All about twins', *Newsweek*, 23 November, 42–8.

Bell, M. (1964), 'Francis Bacon: pioneer in parapsychology', *International Journal of Parapsychology* 6, 199–208.

Blackmore, S. J. and Chamberlain, F. (1993), 'ESP and thought concordance in twins: a method of comparison', *Journal of the Society for Psychical Research* 59 (831), 89–96.

Bohm, D. (1980), *Wholeness and the Implicate Order*, London: Routledge & Kegan Paul.

Bohm, E. R. (1984) *Nonverbal Communication Between Individuals Who Share a Close Emotional Bond: 'ESP' Communication*. PhD thesis, Columbia University Teachers College. *Dissertation Abstracts International*; 1984, 45(08B), 2669.

Campbell, H. (1995), *Two to Begin With*, Pittsburgh: Dorrance.

Carrington, H. (1919), *Psychical Phenomena and the War*. New York: Dodd, Mead.

Charlesworth, E. A. (1975), *Psi and the imaginary dream*. Research in Parapsychology 1974, 85–9.

Conway, A. V. (1988), 'The research game: a view from the field', *Complementary Medical Research* 3 (8), 29–36.

Cooper, C. (1997), *Twins and Multiple Births*, London: Vermilion.

Corliss, W. R. (ed.) (1982), *The Unfathomed Mind: a Handbook of Unusual Mental Phenomena*, Glen Arm: The Sourcebook Project.

Crowe, C. (1848), *The Night-Side of Nature, or Ghosts and Ghost-Seers*, London: T. C. Newby.

Dingwall, E. J. (1967), *Abnormal Hypnotic Phenomena*, vol.1, London: Churchill.

Dixon, J. (1824), *The Twin Brothers*, 5th edition.

Duane, T. D. and Behrendt, T. (1965), 'Extrasensory electroencephalographic induction between identical twins', *Science*, 15 October, 367.

Dumas, A. (1988), *Les frères corses*, Ajaccio: La Marge éditions.

Einstein, A., Podolsky, B. and Rosen, N. (1935), 'Can quantum-mechanical description of physical reality be considered complete?' *Physical Review* 47, 777–80.

Esser, A., Etter, T. L. and Chamberlain, W. B. (1967), 'Preliminary report: physiological concomitants of "communication" between isolated subjects', *International Journal of Parapsychology* 9(1), 53–6.

France, G. A. and Hogan, R. A. (1973), 'Thought concordance in twins and siblings and associated personality variables', *Psychological Reports* 32, 707–10.

Gaddis, V. and Gaddis, M. (1972), *The Curious World of Twins*, New York: Hawthorn.

Galton, F. (1883) *Enquiries into Human Faculty*, London: Macmillan.

Gărdescu, D. (1993) 'Doi frați gemeni ucid în aceeași, la aceeași oră' ['Two twin brothers kill on the same day, at the same time'], *Dracula*, September.

Gavilán Fontanet, F. (1976), 'Los gemelos y su enigma de comunicación psíquica', *Psi Comunicación* 2(3–4) 47–52.

Geddes, A. C. (1937), 'A Voice from the Grandstand', *Edinburgh Medical Journal* N.S.IV. 44 (6), 365–84.

Geddes, A. C. (1952), *The Forging of a Family*, London: Faber & Faber.

BIBLIOGRAPHY

Goswami, A. (2001), *Physics of the Soul*, Charlottesville: Hampton Roads.

Gribbin, J. (1995), *Schrödinger's Kittens and the Search for Reality*. London: Weidenfeld & Nicolson.

Grinberg-Zylberbaum, J. (1994), 'The syntergic theory', *Frontier Perspectives* 4(1) 25–30.

Grinberg-Zylberbaum, J., Delaflor, M., Attie, L. and Goswami, A. (1994), 'The E-P-R paradox in the brain – the transferred potential', *Physics Essays*, 7(4) 422–8.

Gummer, S. (1963), *The Chavasse Twins*, London: Hodder & Stoughton.

Gurney, E., Myers, F. W. H. and Podmore, F. (1886), *Phantasms of the Living*, London: Trübner.

Inglis, B. (1990), *Coincidence*, London: Hutchinson.

Inglis, B. (1992), *Natural and Supernatural*, Bridport: Prism.

Josephson, B. D. (2001), Letter, the *Observer*, 8 October.

Jung, C. G. (1963), *Memories, Dreams, Reflections* (A. Jaffé, ed.). New York: Pantheon.

Jung, C. G. (1972), *Synchronicity. An Acausal Connecting Principle*, London: Routledge & Kegan Paul.

Kray, R. (1991), *Born Fighter*, London: Arrow.

Koestler, A. (1972), *The Roots of Coincidence*. London: Hutchinson.

Koestler, A. (1986), *The Sleepwalkers*, London: Penguin.

Kubis, J. F. and Rouke, F. L. (1937), 'An experimental investigation of telepathic phenomena in twins', *Journal of Parapsychology* 1(3) 163–71.

Lorimer, D. (1999), 'Distant Feelings', *Network* 71, December.

McEvoy, J. P. and Zarate, O. (1996), *Quantum Theory for Beginners*, Trumpington: Icon.

McWhirter, N. (1976), *Ross. The Story of a Shared Life*, London: Churchill.

Matthews, R. (2001), 'I think, therefore I am subatomically entangled', *Sunday Telegraph*, 25 February.

M[edhurst], R. G. (1968), 'Notes and Notices', *Journal of the Society for Psychical Research*, June, 317–9.

Milton, R. (1994), *Forbidden Science*, London: Fourth Estate.

Mitchell, J. L. (1981), *Out-of-Body Experiences*, Wellingborough: Turnstone Press.

Montgomery, R. (1982), *A Search for the Truth*, New York: Fawcett Crest.

Nash, C. B. and Buzby, D. E. (1965), 'Extrasensory perception of identical and fraternal twins: comparison of clairvoyance test scores', *Journal of Heredity* 56(2), 52–4.

Newman, H. H. (1942), *Twins and Super-Twins*, London: Hutchinson.

Nicol, B. and Nicol, J. F. (1957), 'Buried alive – saved by telepathy', *Tomorrow*, Spring, 9–13.

Nicol, J. F. and Nicol, B. (1958), 'Investigation of a curious "hunch"', *Journal of the American Society for Psychical Research*, January, 24–34.

Oppenheim J. (1985), *The Other World*, Cambridge: University Press.

Ostrander, S. and Schroeder, L. (1971), *Psychic Discoveries Behind the Iron Curtain*, New York: Bantam Books.

Puharich, A. (1973), *Beyond Telepathy*, New York: Anchor Books.

Puységur, Marquis de (1809), *Mémoirs pour servir à l'histoire et l'établissement du magnétisme animal*, Paris: Cellot, 2nd edition.

Radin, D. (1997), *The Conscious Universe*, New York: Harper Edge.

Robichon, F.-H. (1989), 'Contribution à l'étude du phénomène télépathique avec des individus liés par la condition biologique de gémellité monozygote', *Revue française de psychotronique*, 2(1), 19–35.

Rogers, W. C. (1960), 'A study of like pattern formation in twins', *Journal of Parapsychology* 24(1), 69.

Rogo, D. S. (1988), 'The Psychic Warriors', in *Psychic Warfare Fact or Fiction?* (J.White, ed.), Wellingborough: Aquarian Press, 194–200.

Rosambeau, M. (1987), *How Twins Grow Up*, London: The Bodley Head.

Russell, G. W. (AE) (1918), *The Candle of Vision*, Wheaton: Theosophical Publishing House.

Scheinfeld, A. (1967), *Twins and Supertwins*, Philadelphia: J.P.Lippincott, 3rd ed.

Schmeidler, G. (1943), 'Predicting good and bad scores in a clairvoyance experiment: A preliminary report', *Journal of the American Society for Psychical Research* 37, 103–10.

Schnabel, J. (1997), *Remote Viewers: The Secret History of America's Psychic Spies*, New York: Dell.

Schwarz, B. E. (1971), *Parent-Child Telepathy*, New York: Garrett Publications.

Segal, N. (n.d.), 'The myth of twins. Separating the fact from the fiction', Videotape. Altadena: The Skeptics Society.

Sheldrake, R. (1999a), *Dogs That Know When Their Owners Are Coming Home*, London: Hutchinson.

Shields, J. (1962), *Monozygotic twins brought up apart and brought up together*, London: Oxford University Press.

Sieveking, P. (1981), 'One in life and death', *The Unexplained* 59, 1174–7.

Sinclair, U. (1971), *Mental Radio*, New York: Collier Books.

Sommer, R., Osmond, H., and Pancyr, L. (1961), 'Selection of twins for ESP experimentation', *International Journal of Parapsychology* 3(4), 55–73.

Speransky, S. V. (1981), 'Extraordinary transmission of information about starvation', in *Parapsychology in the U.S.S.R.*, (L.Vilenskaya, ed.), 3, 4–11.

Spinelli, E. (1983), *Human Development and Paranormal Cognition*, Unpublished PhD thesis, University of Surrey.

Stuart, C. E. (1946), 'GESP experiments with the free response method', *Journal of Parapsychology* 10(1), 21–35.

Townshend, C. H. (1844), *Facts in Mesmerism*, London: H.Baillière.

Ullman, M., Krippner, S. and Vaughan, A. (1989), *Dream Telepathy*, 2nd ed. Jefferson: McFarland.

Vanderbilt, G. and Furness, T. (1959) *Double Exposure: A Twin Autobiography*, London: Frederick Muller.

Vinogradova, G. (1996), *Saint or Sinner? The Life and Times of Russia's New Rasputin, Anatoly Kashpirovsky*. Glastonbury: Gothic Image.

Warcollier, R. (1938), *Experimental Telepathy*, Boston: Boston Society for Psychic Research.

Watson, A. (1997), 'Quantum Spookiness Wins, Einstein Loses in Photon Test', *Science*, 25 July, 481.

Watson, P. (1984*), Twins. An investigation into the strange coincidences in the lives of separated twins*, London: Sphere Books.

Wilder, I. (1985), Foreword, in *The Journals of Thornton Wilder 1939–1961*, (D. Gallup, ed.) New Haven: Yale University Press.

Williams, R. (1982), 'Twin Dreams', *Science Digest*, 26 November.

Wilkins, H. and Sherman, H. (1971), *Thoughts Through Space*, London: Frederick Muller.

Wright, L. (1997*), Twins. Genes, Environment and the Mystery of Identity*, London: Weidenfeld & Nicolson.

Zohar, D. (1990), *The Quantum Self*, London: Bloomsbury.

Zorab, G. (1978), 'Reports from other countries: Spain', *Journal of the Society for Psychical Research*, March, 746–8.

INDEX

INDEX

INDEX